Mastering Emotions: A Guide to Emotional Intelligence and Resilience

Uncover the 7 Keys to Navigating Conflict and Building Emotional Strength

ALI .H

Understanding Emotional Intelligence: The Foundation of EQ 4

Self-Awareness—The First Step Toward Mastery 27

Mastering Emotional Regulation—Staying Calm Under Pressure 50

The Empathy Advantage—Deepening Connections .. 72

Social Skills—Mastering Emotional Intelligence in Relationships 92

Conflict Resolution—Turning Disagreements into Growth 112

Emotional Resilience—Thriving Amidst Adversity .. 131

Lifelong EQ—Applying Emotional Intelligence for Lasting Success 150

Understanding Emotional Intelligence: The Foundation of EQ

The Basics of Emotional Intelligence

Emotional Intelligence (EQ) is one of those qualities we all think we understand intuitively—after all, we experience emotions every day. However, truly understanding emotional intelligence means grasping not only how we feel but also how those feelings influence our behavior and impact the people around us. In its simplest terms, emotional intelligence is the ability to recognize, understand, manage, and regulate emotions—both our own and those of others. This understanding is not just abstract; it can be incredibly practical in everyday life. By mastering EQ, we develop tools for emotional self-regulation, improve our relationships, and navigate life's challenges with a sense of balance and empathy.

What is Emotional Intelligence?

Emotional intelligence begins with self-awareness, the ability to identify and understand our emotions in the moment. Think about the last time you got really frustrated—maybe it was in traffic or during an argument. Did you stop and recognize that frustration? Most of us don't. We feel the heat rising, we might clench our fists or say something we regret, and the moment passes without our realizing how those emotions were affecting our behavior. Being emotionally intelligent means learning to identify that frustration right when it begins to simmer, understanding why it's happening, and using that information to regulate your response. Instead of honking your horn in anger, you might pause, take a breath, and choose to calm yourself down before reacting.

This ability to recognize and manage emotions is a hallmark of emotional intelligence. But EQ isn't only about handling your own emotions—it's also about understanding others. When you can recognize emotions in someone else, you're able to respond in a way that strengthens relationships rather than weakening them. For example, if a colleague is acting short-tempered at work, instead of snapping back, an emotionally intelligent person might recognize the stress behind their colleague's behavior. They might offer support or simply avoid taking the outburst personally, which can diffuse tension and lead to a more harmonious interaction.

The Core Components of EQ

Psychologist Daniel Goleman popularized the concept of emotional intelligence, breaking it down into five core components: self-awareness, self-regulation, motivation, empathy, and social skills. Each of these components plays a role in how we perceive, interpret, and react to emotions, and they're essential in everyday interactions.

Self-awareness, as mentioned earlier, is the cornerstone of emotional intelligence. It's about recognizing our own emotional states and how they affect our thoughts and actions. People with high self-awareness don't just know when they're feeling sad, angry, or anxious—they understand why they're feeling that way and can articulate their emotions clearly. This awareness can help prevent emotional outbursts or regrettable decisions driven by heightened emotions.

Self-regulation follows naturally from self-awareness. Once we recognize our emotions, we can begin to control them. This doesn't mean suppressing or ignoring feelings; rather, it's about managing emotional responses so they align with long-term goals. Take, for example, a leader who receives critical feedback during a meeting. Instead of reacting defensively or shutting down emotionally, someone with high emotional intelligence would take a moment to process their feelings, maintain their composure, and respond constructively. This ability to control immediate reactions can have a significant impact on professional success and personal well-being.

Motivation in the context of emotional intelligence refers to the inner drive to pursue goals with energy and persistence, often despite emotional obstacles. Those with high EQ are motivated not just by external rewards but by internal values like growth, fulfillment, and the pursuit of long-term success. They can harness their emotions to stay focused even when facing challenges.

Empathy, another critical component, is the ability to understand the emotions of others. Empathy allows us to step into another person's shoes, which can transform how we communicate and resolve conflicts. Imagine a scenario where a friend is going through a difficult time. Without empathy, we might offer generic advice or dismiss their feelings. With empathy, however, we can recognize their emotional experience, offer meaningful support, and strengthen our bond with them.

Finally, **social skills** are the outward manifestation of emotional intelligence. They encompass a range of abilities, from conflict resolution and communication to teamwork and persuasion. People with strong social skills can navigate complex social environments, build meaningful relationships, and manage interactions in ways that benefit everyone involved.

The Science Behind Emotions

While emotional intelligence feels like an abstract concept, it's rooted in the hardwiring of our brains. Emotions arise from interactions between different brain regions, particularly the **amygdala** and the **prefrontal cortex**. The amygdala, often called the brain's emotional center, is responsible for processing emotions like fear, anger, and pleasure. When you encounter a stressful situation, the amygdala is the first part of the brain to react, triggering a flood of emotional responses.

The prefrontal cortex, on the other hand, is responsible for regulating those emotional impulses. This area of the brain helps us process emotions, analyze them logically, and make reasoned decisions. Think of a time when you received upsetting news—perhaps you initially felt a surge of panic or anger (your amygdala's doing), but after a few moments, you managed to calm yourself and think through the situation (the prefrontal cortex stepping in).

The interplay between these two parts of the brain is what allows us to regulate our emotional responses. When we lack emotional intelligence, the amygdala often takes over, leading to impulsive reactions. But by strengthening our EQ, we can train our prefrontal cortex to intervene more effectively, helping us pause, reflect, and respond in a measured way.

EQ vs IQ: Why Emotional Intelligence Matters More

For a long time, IQ (Intelligence Quotient) was seen as the gold standard for predicting success. The belief was that the smarter you were—academically and intellectually—the more likely you were to achieve in life. However, as research into emotional intelligence grew, it became clear that IQ alone doesn't guarantee success. In fact, many people with average IQs outperform those with higher IQs in the real world, thanks to their superior emotional intelligence.

One of the key differences between IQ and EQ is how they function in everyday situations. IQ might help you solve complex problems or excel in technical tasks, but EQ is what allows you to build meaningful relationships, manage stress, and navigate the inevitable challenges that arise in life. Imagine a manager with a high IQ but low emotional intelligence. They might be brilliant at analyzing data or creating strategies, but if they can't communicate effectively, empathize with their team, or manage their own stress, they're likely to struggle as a leader. In contrast, a manager with strong EQ might be able to motivate their team, resolve conflicts smoothly, and create a positive work environment, even if their intellectual abilities aren't as sharp.

Consider a real-world example of EQ at play: In a 2007 study of over 200 companies, researchers found that the most successful leaders were not those with the highest IQs but those with the highest EQs. They demonstrated empathy, self-awareness, and social skills, which allowed them to manage teams effectively, foster loyalty, and drive performance. In fact, emotional intelligence was shown to be twice as important as technical skills and IQ combined when it came to leadership success.

Conclusion

Understanding the basics of emotional intelligence gives us a foundation to navigate life with greater awareness, control, and empathy. While IQ measures cognitive abilities, EQ measures our emotional awareness and social effectiveness. Learning to manage our emotions and understand the emotions of others is a vital life skill that goes beyond academic success—it touches every aspect of our personal and professional lives. Whether we are dealing with stress, leading a team, or building deep relationships, emotional intelligence equips us to handle challenges with grace and resilience, turning emotional insight into positive action.

The Five Pillars of Emotional Intelligence

Emotional intelligence (EQ) is not just a vague concept about "being in touch" with your emotions. It is a set of skills that, when developed, can enhance nearly every aspect of life—from personal relationships to professional success. Daniel Goleman, one of the leading psychologists in the field, identified five essential components, or "pillars," of emotional intelligence: self-awareness, self-regulation, motivation, empathy, and social skills. These pillars are the foundation of emotional intelligence, working together to shape how we manage ourselves and interact with others.

In this section, we will focus on three of these key pillars: self-awareness, self-regulation, and motivation. By understanding and practicing these concepts, we can better navigate our emotional landscape and create a healthier, more productive relationship with our feelings.

Self-Awareness: Understanding Your Emotions and Recognizing Triggers

Self-awareness is the bedrock of emotional intelligence. It's the ability to recognize and understand your own emotions, moods, and the thoughts that drive them. Most of us go through life experiencing emotions without pausing to reflect on them—why we feel a certain way or what is triggering those emotions. But without self-awareness, it's difficult to regulate our responses or understand how our feelings influence our decisions.

Consider a moment when you felt inexplicably irritated—perhaps after a tough day at work or a tense conversation with a friend. Did you pause to reflect on what triggered that emotion? Self-awareness allows you to take that pause, enabling you to ask, "Why am I feeling this way?" By understanding the source of your emotions, you can avoid reacting impulsively and instead choose a more thoughtful response.

For example, imagine someone who constantly finds themselves snapping at their partner after a stressful day. Without self-awareness, they may simply blame their partner or circumstances for their frustration. However, if they develop self-awareness, they may realize the stress from work is the real trigger and can address that issue directly, rather than taking it out on a loved one. This deeper understanding of their emotional state gives them the power to control how they respond to stress and other triggers in their environment.

Self-awareness also extends beyond negative emotions. It helps us understand what brings us joy, motivation, or excitement. Knowing what energizes you—whether it's working on creative projects, spending time with family, or solving challenging problems—allows you to actively seek out those experiences, improving your well-being and life satisfaction.

But self-awareness isn't just about identifying emotions in the moment. It involves understanding long-term patterns in how you feel and react. Keeping an emotional journal, for instance, can be a helpful way to track recurring emotions and uncover the deeper causes behind them. Over time, this practice builds emotional insight and leads to a greater mastery of one's internal world.

Self-Regulation: Managing Your Emotions Effectively Under Pressure

Once you develop self-awareness, the next step in emotional intelligence is self-regulation. This is the ability to manage your emotions, particularly in high-pressure or stressful situations. It's one thing to recognize that you're feeling angry or frustrated—it's another to control how you express that emotion, especially when you're under stress.

Picture a leader in the workplace who regularly deals with high-stakes decisions. It's normal for them to experience stress, anxiety, or even frustration. However, a leader with strong self-regulation doesn't allow those emotions to cloud their judgment or negatively affect their interactions with others. Instead, they pause, breathe, and consider the most productive way to respond. This doesn't mean they suppress their emotions—it means they manage them. They may still feel anxious, but they don't let that anxiety dictate their actions. Instead, they find ways to work through it and make rational decisions.

Self-regulation is crucial in personal relationships as well. In a heated argument with a partner, for example, your immediate instinct might be to say something hurtful or defensive. But self-regulation encourages you to take a step back, recognize the emotions bubbling up, and choose a response that aligns with your values and long-term goals—whether that's maintaining harmony in the relationship or resolving the conflict peacefully.

This ability to regulate emotions under pressure can be developed through a variety of strategies. One practical approach is **the pause**. When you feel yourself becoming overwhelmed, anxious, or angry, give yourself permission to pause before reacting. This moment of reflection gives your brain time to shift from emotional reactivity to a more rational, thoughtful response. Techniques like deep breathing, mindfulness, and even physical activity can help shift your emotional state and prevent impulsive actions.

Over time, self-regulation leads to greater emotional resilience. Rather than being controlled by emotions, you learn to control your response to them, which results in more productive outcomes. This skill is particularly beneficial in professional settings, where emotional control can mean the difference between reacting impulsively and making measured, thoughtful decisions. When self-regulation is practiced consistently, it also enhances your reputation for reliability, trustworthiness, and emotional maturity.

Motivation: Using Emotions to Stay Driven and Achieve Goals

Motivation is a central pillar of emotional intelligence that often gets overlooked. When we think of motivation, we typically think of external rewards: bonuses at work, recognition, or tangible achievements. However, in the context of emotional intelligence, motivation refers to the internal drive that pushes us to pursue our goals, stay resilient in the face of challenges, and continuously strive for improvement, all while harnessing our emotions.

Highly motivated individuals don't just chase after success for the sake of rewards; they are driven by a deeper sense of purpose or fulfillment. This internal motivation often comes from the positive emotions tied to progress and growth. For instance, think of an athlete who spends hours training every day, not just for the trophies, but because they find joy and satisfaction in the process of becoming stronger and faster. That internal drive is a hallmark of high emotional intelligence.

Emotionally intelligent individuals use their emotions to fuel motivation. Take the example of an entrepreneur starting a business. The path is full of obstacles—setbacks, financial worries, rejection—but emotionally intelligent entrepreneurs can channel their emotional reactions into fuel for perseverance.

Instead of letting fear of failure paralyze them, they might turn it into excitement about what could be. Instead of dwelling on a disappointment, they focus on the lessons learned and use those insights to keep pushing forward.

One of the most significant aspects of motivation in emotional intelligence is the ability to remain optimistic, even in the face of adversity. Optimism doesn't mean ignoring the challenges or pretending everything is fine—it means maintaining hope and continuing to work toward a goal, even when the going gets tough. This emotional resilience is a key driver of long-term success.

Motivation is also deeply connected to emotional regulation. People who can manage their emotions are better equipped to maintain focus on their goals. They don't allow frustration, boredom, or self-doubt to derail their progress. Instead, they use their emotional awareness to stay aligned with what truly matters to them, whether that's professional success, personal growth, or strong relationships.

To foster emotional motivation, it's helpful to identify what emotionally drives you. Is it the joy of creativity, the fulfillment of helping others, or the satisfaction of personal achievement? Once you recognize these sources of emotional energy, you can tap into them during difficult times to stay on track. Reflecting on why a goal matters to you personally can reignite your passion when obstacles arise.

Conclusion

The five pillars of emotional intelligence—self-awareness, self-regulation, motivation, empathy, and social skills—are interconnected elements that shape how we navigate the emotional landscape of life. By focusing on the first three pillars—self-awareness, self-regulation, and motivation—we can lay a strong foundation for emotional growth. Through self-awareness, we gain insight into our emotions and the triggers behind them. Through self-regulation, we learn to manage our emotional responses effectively, especially under pressure. And through motivation, we discover how to harness our emotions to stay driven and focused on our goals. Together, these skills equip us to face challenges with greater emotional clarity and resilience, enhancing both our personal and professional lives.

The Interpersonal Aspects of EQ

Emotional intelligence (EQ) is often thought of as an internal skill—a way of managing our own emotions. But a key part of EQ is its impact on our relationships with others. The ability to understand and manage emotions extends beyond ourselves and plays a crucial role in how we connect, communicate, and resolve conflicts with others. This interpersonal aspect of EQ can make the difference between thriving relationships and strained, conflict-ridden ones.

In this section, we will explore three key interpersonal components of emotional intelligence: empathy, social skills, and conflict resolution. Each of these skills builds on the emotional awareness and regulation we've already discussed, but they add another layer of complexity as they require us to navigate not just our own emotions but those of the people around us.

Empathy: Developing the Ability to Understand and Share the Feelings of Others

Empathy is often described as the ability to put ourselves in someone else's shoes. It's the capacity to understand and share the feelings of others, which is a cornerstone of emotional intelligence. But empathy goes beyond simply acknowledging someone else's emotions—it requires truly feeling what they feel and responding in a way that shows understanding and compassion. This ability to connect emotionally with others is critical for building strong, healthy relationships.

Think about the last time you had a difficult conversation with a friend who was going through a tough time. Maybe they were feeling overwhelmed by work or upset about a personal issue. In that moment, you had a choice: you could have brushed off their feelings, offered quick advice, or taken the time to really listen and understand what they were experiencing. True empathy would guide you to the latter approach, where you focus on what they're feeling without trying to "fix" things immediately. By listening, validating their emotions, and offering support, you create a space where they feel understood and valued.

Empathy doesn't always come naturally. Many of us are quick to judge, offer solutions, or shift the focus back to ourselves. But developing empathy means learning to set aside our immediate reactions and instead focus on the emotional needs of the other person. This can be especially difficult in situations where we disagree with someone or don't fully understand their perspective. However, even in these challenging moments, empathy allows us to bridge the emotional gap between ourselves and others.

For example, imagine you're a manager at work, and an employee approaches you looking stressed and frustrated about a project. Without empathy, you might respond with impatience or push them to meet their deadlines. But an empathetic response would involve recognizing the stress they're feeling, asking what's going on, and helping them find a way to manage the pressure. This response doesn't just address their immediate concern—it builds trust and strengthens your relationship, creating a more positive and supportive work environment.

Empathy is not just about being "nice." It's a powerful tool for effective communication and relationship-building. When others feel seen and understood, they're more likely to open up, collaborate, and share their thoughts and feelings openly. This creates a deeper connection and often leads to better outcomes, whether in personal relationships, the workplace, or social settings.

Social Skills: Building Better Relationships Through Emotional Understanding

Social skills are the practical expression of emotional intelligence in our interactions with others. They encompass a broad range of abilities, from communication and teamwork to persuasion and leadership. At the heart of strong social skills is the ability to understand and manage emotions—both our own and those of others—so that we can navigate relationships effectively.

Good social skills begin with effective communication. People with high EQ know how to express their thoughts and feelings clearly and constructively. They're skilled at reading the emotional cues of others, whether those cues are verbal or nonverbal, and adjusting their communication style accordingly. For example, a socially skilled person can tell when someone is feeling anxious or upset even if that person hasn't said so directly. They'll adjust their tone, body language, or words to address the emotional state of the other person, making the conversation more productive.

Imagine a situation at work where a team is struggling to meet a deadline. A leader with strong social skills will recognize the underlying emotional dynamics within the group—perhaps some members are feeling frustrated, while others are anxious about their performance. Instead of simply pushing the team harder, the leader might address these emotions directly, offering encouragement or breaking down tasks to reduce stress. By acknowledging and addressing the team's emotional needs, the leader can improve morale and productivity.

Social skills also play a key role in building and maintaining relationships. Whether we're dealing with a romantic partner, a family member, or a colleague, the ability to connect emotionally and communicate effectively is essential. For instance, in personal relationships, social skills help us navigate difficult conversations, express our needs without causing conflict, and listen actively to our partner's concerns. In professional settings, these skills enable us to collaborate more effectively, resolve disagreements, and build a positive team environment.

One of the most important social skills is **active listening**—the ability to focus entirely on the speaker, understand their message, and respond thoughtfully. Active listening involves not just hearing the words being said but also paying attention to the emotions behind them. For example, if a colleague is venting about a problem at work, active listening might involve nodding, maintaining eye contact, and reflecting back what they've said to show understanding. This simple act of listening can diffuse tension and help resolve the issue more quickly.

Building strong social skills takes practice, but the rewards are immense. Whether you're trying to form deeper personal connections, lead a team, or resolve a conflict, emotional understanding and communication are at the heart of success.

Conflict Resolution: Navigating Conflicts by Using Emotional Intelligence Strategies

Conflict is an inevitable part of life. Whether in personal relationships, at work, or in social interactions, disagreements and misunderstandings will arise. How we handle these conflicts is a true test of our emotional intelligence. Emotionally intelligent people don't avoid conflict—instead, they use their EQ skills to navigate it in a way that strengthens relationships and resolves issues productively.

One of the key components of emotional intelligence in conflict resolution is **emotional regulation**. When emotions run high during a disagreement, it's easy to let anger or frustration take over, leading to defensive or aggressive responses. But those with high EQ can manage their emotions in the heat of the moment, allowing them to stay calm and focused on finding a solution rather than escalating the conflict. For example, in an argument with a partner, someone with high EQ might feel hurt or angry but instead of reacting impulsively, they'll take a breath, acknowledge their feelings, and approach the conversation with a goal of resolution rather than winning the argument.

Empathy also plays a crucial role in resolving conflicts. By understanding the emotions and perspectives of the other person, we're able to address their concerns more effectively. Take the example of a workplace conflict where two team members disagree on how to approach a project. Without empathy, each person might dig in their heels, refusing to consider the other's point of view. But with empathy, they're more likely to listen to each other, understand the underlying concerns, and find a compromise that meets both of their needs. Empathy doesn't mean agreeing with the other person—it means recognizing their feelings as valid and working from a place of understanding rather than judgment.

A third element of emotional intelligence in conflict resolution is **problem-solving**. Emotionally intelligent people focus on finding solutions rather than dwelling on the conflict itself. Instead of getting stuck in a cycle of blame or frustration, they approach the situation with a collaborative mindset, looking for ways to resolve the issue in a way that benefits everyone involved. This might involve negotiating, compromising, or brainstorming creative solutions to a problem. For example, in a disagreement between colleagues, a solution-focused approach might involve bringing in a mediator, discussing alternative approaches, or agreeing on a trial period for a new idea.

In personal relationships, conflict resolution is equally important. Couples who use emotional intelligence to resolve disagreements are more likely to strengthen their relationship over time. They approach conflicts with empathy, open communication, and a focus on finding common ground, rather than letting anger or resentment fester. Over time, this approach builds trust, improves communication, and deepens emotional intimacy.

Conclusion

The interpersonal aspects of emotional intelligence—empathy, social skills, and conflict resolution—are crucial for building and maintaining strong, healthy relationships. Empathy allows us to understand and share the feelings of others, creating deeper connections. Social skills help us communicate effectively, navigate social dynamics, and build positive relationships. Conflict resolution enables us to handle disagreements with emotional intelligence, focusing on solutions rather than escalation. By developing these interpersonal aspects of EQ, we not only improve our personal and professional relationships but also contribute to a more emotionally intelligent and harmonious world.

Self-Awareness—The First Step Toward Mastery

Recognizing Your Emotional Patterns

Self-awareness is often regarded as the cornerstone of emotional intelligence. It is the first step toward understanding how we think, feel, and act in different situations. At the heart of self-awareness lies the ability to recognize and understand our emotional patterns. These patterns shape our reactions, influence our decisions, and dictate how we interact with the world around us. But without conscious reflection, these patterns can remain hidden, driving us on autopilot. Developing self-awareness involves taking the time to reflect on our emotions, identify triggers that set them off, and expand our emotional vocabulary to better understand what we're truly feeling.

The Power of Reflection: How Journaling and Self-Assessment Help Identify Emotional Patterns

Reflection is an essential practice when it comes to understanding emotional patterns. It is through reflection that we begin to connect the dots between our emotional responses and the situations that prompt them. Without deliberate reflection, emotions can feel like random, uncontrollable forces, but with time and attention, patterns emerge. The more we reflect, the more we can identify trends in how we react to certain circumstances, people, or environments.

One of the most effective tools for reflection is **journaling**. Journaling allows us to slow down and capture our thoughts and emotions on paper, offering clarity that we often miss in the moment. It provides an opportunity to look back and see recurring themes in our emotional experiences. For instance, you might notice that every time you have a meeting with a particular colleague, you feel anxious or defensive. Journaling about these experiences can help you uncover what about the interaction triggers that response. Perhaps it's the colleague's tone, the way they question your ideas, or something deeper related to past experiences with authority figures. By writing down your thoughts and emotions, you can explore these patterns and gain insight into your triggers.

Let's take the story of Sarah, a marketing manager who always found herself overwhelmed before big presentations. She felt dread and anxiety in the days leading up to these events, but she didn't understand why. It wasn't until she began journaling regularly that she uncovered a pattern: her anxiety wasn't about the presentation itself, but about a fear of judgment. Sarah realized she feared not being seen as competent, which stemmed from a past experience where her ideas were dismissed. Through reflection, Sarah could identify her fear of judgment as the root cause of her anxiety. With this awareness, she was able to reframe her approach to presentations, focusing on her preparation rather than worrying about others' opinions.

Self-assessment doesn't always have to take the form of journaling. It can also involve taking moments throughout the day to pause and ask yourself, "What am I feeling right now, and why?" These brief moments of reflection offer real-time insights into your emotional state, helping you build a habit of self-awareness. Over time, these regular check-ins can reveal the emotional patterns that drive your day-to-day interactions, helping you respond to situations with more intentionality.

Identifying Emotional Triggers: Recognizing What Sparks Intense Emotional Responses

One of the most critical aspects of self-awareness is recognizing your **emotional triggers**. Triggers are external stimuli—situations, words, or behaviors—that spark an intense emotional response. They can be anything from someone raising their voice to being stuck in traffic, but what makes them significant is the way they affect you emotionally. Identifying your triggers allows you to take control of your reactions, rather than being controlled by them.

To better understand emotional triggers, consider the story of James, a software developer who often found himself feeling angry and frustrated during meetings. He noticed that whenever someone questioned his work or suggested improvements, he became defensive. His immediate emotional response was to feel attacked, even if the feedback was constructive. Over time, James realized that these moments triggered an old wound related to feeling undervalued in a previous job. By identifying this pattern, James was able to approach feedback with greater objectivity, recognizing that the emotional intensity he experienced wasn't about the present moment, but about past experiences.

When you start identifying your own emotional triggers, it's important to ask yourself: What are the specific situations that make me feel out of control emotionally? Are there certain people or topics that consistently bring up strong feelings of anger, fear, sadness, or even joy? Once you pinpoint these situations, you can begin to unravel the underlying causes of your emotional responses.

For example, you might notice that you feel anxious whenever your boss asks you for a last-minute update on a project. Upon deeper reflection, you might realize that it's not the task itself that causes anxiety, but the feeling of being unprepared or fearing criticism. Recognizing this trigger allows you to address the root cause of the anxiety, whether it's improving your preparation habits or learning to manage the discomfort of receiving feedback.

Triggers are often tied to unresolved past experiences or fears. By identifying them, you gain the power to address the underlying issue and shift your emotional response. Instead of being blindsided by intense feelings, you can approach these situations with greater emotional clarity and control.

The Importance of Emotional Vocabulary: Expanding Your Language to Better Articulate and Understand Emotions

One of the most overlooked aspects of self-awareness is the role of **emotional vocabulary**. The words we use to describe our emotions shape how we understand and process them. When we have a limited emotional vocabulary, we tend to oversimplify our feelings, which can prevent us from truly understanding what's going on beneath the surface. Expanding our emotional vocabulary allows us to articulate our emotions more precisely, leading to better self-awareness and emotional management.

Consider the difference between saying, "I'm stressed" versus, "I'm feeling overwhelmed because I don't have enough time to finish everything I need to do." The first statement is vague and doesn't offer much insight into what's really happening, while the second statement provides clarity. It breaks down the emotion and connects it to a specific cause, making it easier to address. The more specific you can be with your emotions, the easier it is to take action to manage them.

Take Maria, for example, a busy mother and project manager. Whenever she felt irritable or short-tempered, she would chalk it up to being "stressed."

But after working with a coach to expand her emotional vocabulary, she began to distinguish between feeling anxious, frustrated, and overwhelmed. She realized that "stress" was a blanket term she had been using to describe several different emotions. By breaking these emotions down into more specific terms, Maria was able to identify that her frustration often stemmed from feeling unappreciated at home, while her anxiety was related to tight deadlines at work. This newfound clarity helped her address the root causes of her emotions rather than lumping everything under a single label of stress.

Developing a rich emotional vocabulary isn't just about labeling negative emotions. It also allows you to appreciate and articulate positive emotions with greater depth. For instance, instead of saying you feel "happy," you might describe your feelings as "content," "excited," or "grateful." Each word carries a different nuance, helping you understand and savor the full range of your emotional experiences.

Expanding your emotional vocabulary can be as simple as learning new words for different emotions and practicing using them in your daily life. You might start by reading through a list of emotion words or observing how characters in books, movies, or conversations express their feelings. The goal is to move beyond broad, generic terms like "happy," "sad," or "angry," and develop a more nuanced understanding of what you're feeling at any given moment.

When you can accurately name your emotions, you gain greater control over how you respond to them. You move from simply reacting to your feelings to making deliberate, informed choices about how to manage them. For instance, recognizing the difference between feeling "frustrated" and feeling "disrespected" helps you decide whether the best course of action is to take a break and cool off or to address a deeper issue with someone in your life.

Conclusion

Recognizing your emotional patterns is an essential step toward developing self-awareness and, by extension, emotional intelligence. Through practices like reflection and journaling, we can uncover the recurring emotional responses that shape our behavior. By identifying emotional triggers, we gain the ability to anticipate and manage intense emotional reactions, leading to more thoughtful and intentional responses. Finally, by expanding our emotional vocabulary, we deepen our understanding of our own emotions, allowing us to articulate and process them more effectively.

By making self-awareness a priority in your life, you're not just gaining insight into your own emotional world—you're taking the first step toward greater emotional mastery. This foundation of understanding will support you in all aspects of emotional intelligence, from regulating your emotions to building stronger, more empathetic relationships with others. Ultimately, recognizing your emotional patterns empowers you to navigate life with greater clarity, resilience, and purpose.

Cultivating Mindfulness for Self-Awareness

Self-awareness is not a static trait; it's a skill that can be developed over time through intentional practices. One of the most powerful tools for cultivating self-awareness is mindfulness. Mindfulness allows us to step back from the rush of everyday life and observe our thoughts, feelings, and physical sensations without judgment. By practicing mindfulness, we can better understand our emotional patterns, stay grounded in the present moment, and respond to life's challenges with greater clarity and calm. This section explores how mindful awareness, present-moment living, and breathing techniques can help us deepen our self-awareness and emotional intelligence.

Mindful Awareness: Using Mindfulness Techniques to Become More Aware of Thoughts and Feelings

Mindful awareness is the practice of paying attention to our thoughts and feelings as they arise, without being swept away by them. It involves creating a space between stimulus and response, where we can observe our emotional and mental states rather than reacting impulsively. This practice is essential for developing self-awareness because it allows us to become more conscious of the internal dialogue that drives our behavior.

Consider the story of Alex, a sales manager who struggled with sudden bouts of frustration during team meetings. Whenever one of his employees failed to meet expectations, Alex would feel a wave of irritation rise up, often leading to curt responses or criticism. After attending a mindfulness workshop, Alex began practicing mindful awareness. Instead of reacting immediately when he felt frustrated, he started pausing to notice the feeling as it emerged. He would silently acknowledge the frustration, noting it with curiosity instead of judgment. This practice of mindful awareness helped Alex see that his irritation wasn't just about his employees' performance—it was rooted in his own fear of failure and perfectionism.

Mindfulness allows us to observe emotions like frustration, anger, sadness, or anxiety with a sense of detachment. We start to see them as passing states rather than permanent parts of our identity. This perspective shift gives us the freedom to respond to emotions in a way that aligns with our values, rather than letting them dictate our actions.

One way to practice mindful awareness is to set aside time each day for mindfulness meditation. In this practice, you sit quietly and focus on your breath or a particular sensation, allowing thoughts and emotions to come and go without engaging with them. Over time, this practice trains your mind to stay present and notice when emotions or unhelpful thoughts arise.

Another practical way to integrate mindful awareness into daily life is to take "mindfulness breaks." Throughout the day, take a moment to pause, close your eyes, and tune into your current emotional state. Ask yourself: "What am I feeling right now?" "What thoughts are running through my mind?" This simple practice of checking in helps you cultivate the habit of emotional awareness, even in the midst of a busy day.

Living in the Present Moment: Reducing Anxiety by Focusing on the Now, Not the Past or Future

One of the core principles of mindfulness is living in the present moment. Many of us spend much of our time either dwelling on the past or worrying about the future, which can lead to heightened anxiety and stress. Learning to anchor ourselves in the present helps reduce this mental clutter and allows us to fully experience life as it unfolds. This focus on the present moment is a critical component of self-awareness, as it enables us to notice our emotional and physical responses in real-time, rather than being lost in rumination or anticipation.

Imagine Lisa, a marketing director who constantly found herself worrying about upcoming deadlines and replaying past mistakes in her head. She was always tense, feeling the weight of both past regrets and future anxieties. During a mindfulness retreat, Lisa learned about the practice of "being in the now." She began using mindfulness techniques to focus on what was happening in the present, instead of allowing her mind to drift into the future or past. For example, when Lisa felt overwhelmed about an upcoming presentation, she would gently bring her focus back to the task at hand—preparing her slides or practicing her delivery—rather than getting lost in fears of what might go wrong.

Living in the present moment is not about ignoring the past or future altogether, but about recognizing that neither exists in the here and now. By focusing on what is happening in the present, we free ourselves from the grip of regret or worry and can fully engage with our current experience.

To practice living in the present moment, start by paying attention to the small details of your environment. When you're eating, notice the taste and texture of the food. When you're walking, feel the sensation of your feet hitting the ground. When you're talking with someone, focus entirely on the conversation without letting your mind wander to other concerns. These simple practices help train your brain to stay grounded in the now.

For people who experience anxiety, this practice can be especially powerful. Anxiety often stems from thoughts about what might happen in the future—whether that's fear of failure, uncertainty about a decision, or worry about how others will react. By cultivating present-moment awareness, you can interrupt the cycle of anxious thoughts and return to the safety and stability of the present.

Mindfulness also helps us respond more calmly to stressful situations. When you're fully present, you're less likely to be swept away by the rush of emotions that often accompany stress. You can recognize the stress as it arises, acknowledge it without judgment, and decide how you want to respond.

Breathing Techniques to Ground Yourself: Practical Exercises for Managing Emotional Responses in Real Time

One of the simplest yet most effective mindfulness practices is conscious breathing. Breathing techniques are powerful tools for grounding yourself in the present moment and managing emotional responses in real-time. When emotions run high, our breathing often becomes shallow and rapid, which can amplify feelings of stress or anxiety. By learning how to control our breath, we can calm our nervous system, reduce the intensity of emotional reactions, and stay centered.

Consider Daniel, a lawyer who often found himself overwhelmed in high-pressure situations, such as when presenting in court or negotiating with clients. Daniel's heart would race, his hands would shake, and his mind would go blank. After being introduced to mindful breathing exercises, he started practicing deep breathing whenever he felt these signs of anxiety coming on. During a particularly stressful negotiation, Daniel noticed his heart rate rising, so he discreetly took a few deep, slow breaths, inhaling through his nose and exhaling through his mouth. Within moments, he felt his body relax, and he was able to think more clearly and approach the negotiation with confidence.

Breathing exercises can be used anytime, anywhere, to regain control over your emotional state. One simple technique is **4-7-8 breathing**. To practice this, inhale through your nose for a count of four, hold your breath for a count of seven, and exhale through your mouth for a count of eight. This exercise activates the parasympathetic nervous system, which helps calm the body and reduce feelings of stress or anxiety.

Another effective breathing technique is **box breathing**, which is often used by athletes and high-performance professionals to manage stress. To do this, inhale for four counts, hold for four counts, exhale for four counts, and hold again for four counts before repeating the cycle. Box breathing helps regulate your breath, slows your heart rate, and allows you to regain focus during emotionally charged moments.

Breathing techniques are particularly useful because they can be employed in real time, whether you're in a meeting, dealing with a difficult conversation, or managing a personal conflict. By focusing on your breath, you can anchor yourself in the present moment, reduce the intensity of your emotional response, and create space to choose how to respond rather than react.

Beyond immediate emotional regulation, breathing exercises also contribute to long-term emotional balance. Regular practice of conscious breathing helps strengthen the connection between the mind and body, allowing you to develop greater emotional resilience over time.

Conclusion

Cultivating mindfulness is an essential practice for enhancing self-awareness and emotional intelligence. Through mindful awareness, we learn to observe our thoughts and emotions without judgment, gaining deeper insight into our internal world. By focusing on the present moment, we reduce anxiety and stress, allowing ourselves to fully engage with the experiences at hand. Finally, by incorporating breathing techniques, we can manage emotional responses in real-time, staying grounded and centered in even the most challenging situations.

Mindfulness is not just a tool for moments of crisis—it's a daily practice that builds emotional resilience and self-awareness over time. By integrating mindfulness into your life, you will not only gain greater control over your emotional responses, but also develop a deeper understanding of yourself, leading to more intentional, thoughtful, and emotionally intelligent interactions with the world around you.

How Self-Awareness Improves Decision-Making

Self-awareness is not merely about understanding ourselves better—it's also about enhancing our ability to make more informed and balanced decisions. The decisions we make, from daily choices to major life changes, are deeply influenced by our emotions. While emotions can sometimes cloud our judgment, a heightened self-awareness allows us to navigate these emotional currents effectively. By recognizing the emotional drivers behind our decisions, identifying cognitive biases, and using our emotions as a guide rather than a hindrance, we can make decisions that are not only more rational but also more aligned with our true needs and values.

Emotions and Decision-Making: Understanding the Emotional Drivers Behind Decisions

Emotions play a significant role in decision-making, often steering us in ways that our rational mind might not predict. They can act as both a compass and a potential distraction, influencing how we perceive options and weigh outcomes. To understand how emotions affect decision-making, consider the story of Emily, a young professional who was offered two job opportunities: one with a high salary but a demanding schedule, and another with lower pay but a better work-life balance. Emily felt a strong emotional pull toward the higher-paying job, driven by the excitement of increased financial security and status. However, upon closer self-reflection, she realized that her initial emotional response was overshadowing her long-term needs for balance and personal well-being.

In this case, Emily's emotions were initially guiding her toward the job that seemed more attractive on the surface. Yet, by practicing self-awareness, she was able to recognize that her excitement was masking deeper concerns about job stress and personal happiness. This realization allowed Emily to make a more thoughtful decision that aligned with her long-term values and personal goals, rather than simply following an emotionally charged impulse.

Emotions can provide valuable insights into what truly matters to us and what we are passionate about. They can help us identify our core values and desires, which are crucial for making decisions that lead to genuine satisfaction and fulfillment. However, without self-awareness, we may not fully understand the emotions driving our choices, leading us to make decisions that are reactive rather than reflective.

To enhance your decision-making process, practice tuning into your emotional responses and asking yourself what they are signaling about your needs and values. For instance, if you feel a strong aversion to a certain option, explore whether this reaction is due to fear, past experiences, or a genuine misalignment with your values.

Recognizing Cognitive Biases: How Emotions Distort Judgment and How to Correct for Them

Cognitive biases are systematic patterns of deviation from norm or rationality in judgment, and they are often influenced by our emotions. These biases can distort our decision-making processes, leading us to make choices based on incomplete or skewed information. Self-awareness helps us recognize these biases and counteract their effects, leading to more balanced and rational decisions.

Consider Tom, a business executive who often relied on the advice of his closest colleagues when making important decisions. Over time, Tom noticed that he was increasingly falling prey to the **confirmation bias**—the tendency to seek out information that confirms his existing beliefs and ignore evidence that contradicts them. Tom's emotional attachment to his colleagues' opinions and his desire for agreement led him to overlook alternative perspectives that could have been beneficial.

By becoming more self-aware, Tom was able to identify this cognitive bias and take steps to correct it. He started actively seeking out diverse viewpoints and considering dissenting opinions before making decisions. This approach allowed Tom to make more informed choices, as he was no longer constrained by his emotional attachment to familiar perspectives.

Common cognitive biases influenced by emotions include **overconfidence bias** (where excessive confidence in our judgments leads to poor decisions) and **availability heuristic** (where recent or vivid memories disproportionately influence our judgments). Self-awareness involves recognizing when these biases are at play and taking deliberate steps to counteract them.

One practical way to counter cognitive biases is to actively challenge your initial judgments. For example, if you find yourself leaning toward a particular decision based on a strong emotional reaction, ask yourself: What evidence do I have to support this choice? What evidence might contradict it? By critically evaluating both sides, you can mitigate the impact of emotional biases on your decision-making.

Making Emotionally Informed Choices:
Using Emotions as a Guide, Not a Barrier,
to Make Better Decisions

While emotions can sometimes cloud our judgment, they can also be a valuable source of information when making decisions. Self-awareness allows us to use emotions as a guide rather than a barrier, helping us to navigate choices in a way that aligns with our values and goals.

Take the example of Julia, an entrepreneur who faced a difficult decision about expanding her business into a new market. Julia felt a strong emotional pull toward the expansion due to her excitement about the growth opportunities and her desire to achieve long-term success. However, she also felt anxious about the potential risks involved. By practicing self-awareness, Julia was able to recognize that her excitement was driving her to overlook some of the risks, while her anxiety was highlighting valid concerns that needed to be addressed.

Julia used this emotional insight to make a more balanced decision. She acknowledged her enthusiasm for the expansion but also took the time to carefully evaluate the risks and develop a strategy to mitigate them. This approach allowed her to make an informed decision that considered both her emotional motivations and the practical realities of the situation.

To make emotionally informed choices, start by acknowledging and reflecting on your emotions in the decision-making process. Ask yourself how your emotions might be influencing your perceptions of the options available to you. Are you feeling particularly optimistic or pessimistic about a choice? How might these emotions be affecting your judgment?

Additionally, consider how your emotional response aligns with your long-term goals and values. Emotions can provide valuable clues about what is truly important to you. For instance, if you're excited about an opportunity but also feeling apprehensive, this may indicate that the opportunity aligns with your goals but also presents challenges that need to be addressed.

By integrating your emotional insights with rational analysis, you can make decisions that are not only informed by your emotions but also grounded in practical considerations. This balanced approach helps ensure that your decisions reflect both your emotional needs and your practical realities.

Conclusion

Self-awareness plays a crucial role in enhancing our decision-making abilities. By understanding the emotional drivers behind our decisions, recognizing cognitive biases, and using emotions as a guide rather than a hindrance, we can make more balanced and informed choices. Emotions provide valuable insights into our values and desires, but without self-awareness, they can also lead us astray. By developing a deeper understanding of our emotional patterns and practicing mindfulness, we can navigate decision-making with greater clarity and confidence. This approach allows us to make decisions that not only align with our immediate needs but also support our long-term goals and overall well-being.

Mastering Emotional Regulation—Staying Calm Under Pressure

Controlling Your Reactions

In the fast-paced and often unpredictable world we live in, maintaining control over our emotional reactions is a crucial skill. Emotional regulation involves managing our emotions effectively so that we can respond to situations in a balanced and constructive manner. This ability not only enhances our personal well-being but also improves our interactions with others and our overall effectiveness in various aspects of life. In this section, we will explore key strategies for controlling our reactions, including the Pause Principle, developing emotional flexibility, and leveraging self-talk to manage intense emotions.

The Pause Principle: How to Pause Before Reacting Emotionally in Stressful Situations

The Pause Principle is a fundamental technique for emotional regulation. It involves taking a deliberate pause before responding to a stressful or emotionally charged situation. This pause allows us to step back from our immediate emotional reaction and assess the situation more thoughtfully. By incorporating this pause, we create a space between stimulus and response, which helps prevent knee-jerk reactions that can lead to regret or conflict.

Consider the experience of Jason, a team leader who often found himself reacting impulsively during heated meetings. Whenever a team member challenged his ideas or criticized his decisions, Jason would quickly become defensive, leading to escalated conflicts. Recognizing the need to manage his reactions more effectively, Jason started practicing the Pause Principle. Before responding to criticism or conflict, he would take a deep breath and count to five. This brief moment of reflection allowed him to calm his initial emotional response and choose a more measured and constructive reply.

The Pause Principle can be practiced in various ways. For some, it may involve taking a few deep breaths or counting silently to create a moment of distance from the emotional reaction. For others, it might mean physically stepping away from the situation for a moment or delaying an immediate response until you have had time to think. The key is to create a deliberate gap between the emotional stimulus and your reaction, which helps you respond with greater clarity and intention.

Incorporating the Pause Principle into your daily life requires practice and mindfulness. Start by identifying situations where you tend to react impulsively and consciously remind yourself to pause before responding. Over time, this practice will become more natural, allowing you to handle stress and conflict with greater ease and composure.

Developing Emotional Flexibility: Adapting Quickly to Emotional Challenges and Setbacks

Emotional flexibility is the ability to adapt to changing emotional circumstances and respond to challenges with resilience and composure. It involves recognizing that emotions are dynamic and that our responses must be flexible to meet the demands of different situations. Developing emotional flexibility helps us manage setbacks and challenges more effectively, allowing us to maintain balance and perspective even when faced with adversity.

Take the example of Maria, a project manager who encountered unexpected obstacles in her work. When a key team member unexpectedly left the project, Maria initially felt frustrated and overwhelmed by the disruption. However, rather than letting her emotions derail her progress, she practiced emotional flexibility. She acknowledged her frustration but quickly shifted her focus to finding solutions and adjusting the project plan. By remaining adaptable and open to new approaches, Maria was able to navigate the challenge and keep the project on track.

Emotional flexibility involves several key components: recognizing and accepting your emotions, reframing challenges as opportunities for growth, and being willing to adjust your approach as needed. When faced with setbacks or changes, start by acknowledging your emotional response and understanding its impact. Rather than resisting or denying these feelings, accept them as part of the process and use them as a catalyst for finding solutions.

For instance, if you experience a setback at work, such as a missed deadline or a failed project, use emotional flexibility to reassess the situation and identify alternative strategies. This may involve seeking feedback, revising your goals, or adjusting your plans to better align with the current circumstances. By remaining adaptable and focused on solutions, you can overcome obstacles and continue moving forward with greater resilience.

Developing emotional flexibility also involves being open to feedback and learning from your experiences. When faced with challenges, consider how your responses can be adjusted based on past experiences and feedback from others. This willingness to adapt and learn enhances your ability to handle future emotional challenges with greater ease.

The Role of Self-Talk in Regulation: Using Positive Internal Dialogue to Calm Intense Emotions

Self-talk refers to the internal dialogue we have with ourselves and plays a crucial role in emotional regulation. Positive self-talk involves using affirmations and constructive thoughts to manage intense emotions and maintain a balanced perspective. By shaping our internal dialogue, we can influence our emotional state and navigate stressful situations more effectively.

Consider the story of Brian, a high-pressure sales executive who often experienced stress and anxiety during important client meetings. Brian found that his internal self-talk was often negative, with thoughts like, "I'm going to mess this up," or "They're going to think I'm incompetent." This negative self-talk amplified his stress and hindered his performance.

To address this, Brian began practicing positive self-talk. Before each meeting, he would repeat affirmations such as, "I am prepared and capable," and "I have the skills and knowledge to succeed." By consciously shifting his internal dialogue to a more positive and supportive tone, Brian was able to manage his stress more effectively and approach each meeting with greater confidence and composure.

Positive self-talk can help regulate emotions by reinforcing a constructive mindset and reducing negative self-judgment. When faced with intense emotions, such as anxiety or frustration, use self-talk to remind yourself of your strengths, capabilities, and past successes. For example, if you're feeling overwhelmed by a challenging task, use self-talk to reassure yourself that you've faced similar challenges before and that you have the skills to overcome them.

In addition to positive affirmations, self-talk can involve reframing negative thoughts and focusing on problem-solving. If you catch yourself engaging in negative self-talk, challenge those thoughts by asking, "Is this thought accurate?" "What evidence do I have to support or refute it?" Reframing negative thoughts in a more balanced and realistic way helps you manage your emotions and approach situations with a clearer and more rational mindset.

Conclusion

Controlling our emotional reactions is a vital aspect of emotional regulation and overall well-being. By implementing the Pause Principle, we create a space between stimulus and response, allowing us to manage our reactions with greater clarity and intention. Developing emotional flexibility enables us to adapt to changing circumstances and setbacks, maintaining resilience and balance in the face of challenges. Additionally, positive self-talk helps regulate intense emotions by fostering a constructive and supportive internal dialogue.

Mastering these strategies empowers us to navigate stressful situations with greater composure and effectiveness. As we become more adept at controlling our reactions, adapting to emotional challenges, and managing our self-talk, we enhance our ability to stay calm under pressure and make decisions that align with our values and goals. Through consistent practice and self-awareness, we can develop the emotional regulation skills needed to thrive in both our personal and professional lives.

Building Emotional Resilience

Building emotional resilience is essential for navigating life's inevitable ups and downs with strength and poise. Resilience allows us to recover from adversity, manage stress effectively, and maintain our emotional equilibrium even in the face of significant challenges. This section delves into how strengthening mental fortitude, shifting perspectives, and balancing emotions in high-stress situations contribute to building emotional resilience.

Strengthening Your Mental Fortitude: Techniques to Bounce Back from Adversity and Emotional Strain

Mental fortitude is the psychological strength that enables us to persevere through adversity and bounce back from setbacks. Developing mental fortitude involves building resilience through various techniques that help us manage emotional strain and recover from difficult situations.

Consider the experience of Sarah, a small business owner who faced significant challenges when her company experienced a major financial setback. Initially, Sarah felt overwhelmed and disheartened by the magnitude of the problem. However, she realized that her ability to recover and move forward depended on her mental fortitude.

Sarah began practicing several techniques to build her resilience. She adopted a proactive approach to problem-solving, focusing on what actions she could take to address the financial issues rather than dwelling on the setbacks. She also engaged in regular self-care practices, such as exercise and mindfulness, to maintain her emotional well-being. Additionally, Sarah sought support from a mentor, who provided guidance and encouragement during the difficult period.

Strengthening mental fortitude involves developing a mindset that views challenges as opportunities for growth rather than insurmountable obstacles. Techniques such as setting realistic goals, practicing self-compassion, and maintaining a positive outlook contribute to building this resilience.

Setting realistic goals helps us break down larger challenges into manageable steps, making it easier to navigate adversity. For example, if you're facing a significant work-related project, break it down into smaller tasks and focus on completing them one at a time. This approach reduces feelings of overwhelm and fosters a sense of accomplishment as you make progress.

Practicing self-compassion involves treating yourself with kindness and understanding when faced with difficulties. Instead of being self-critical, acknowledge that setbacks are a normal part of life and that you are doing your best under the circumstances. Self-compassion helps you maintain a positive mindset and recover more quickly from emotional strain.

Maintaining a positive outlook involves focusing on the aspects of a situation that you can control and finding meaning in the challenges you face. For instance, if you experience a job loss, view it as an opportunity to explore new career paths or pursue personal interests that you may not have had the chance to before. By framing challenges in a positive light, you build resilience and strengthen your ability to bounce back from adversity.

The Power of Perspective: Shifting Your Perspective to Overcome Emotional Overwhelm

Perspective plays a crucial role in how we experience and manage emotional overwhelm. By shifting our perspective, we can change how we perceive challenges and reduce their emotional impact. This shift helps us approach difficulties with greater clarity and composure, enabling us to handle stress more effectively.

Take the example of Jack, a college student who felt overwhelmed by the pressure of his academic workload and personal responsibilities. Jack's initial perspective was that his situation was unmanageable and that he was falling behind in every area of his life. However, he decided to shift his perspective by focusing on the aspects of his situation that he could control and reframing his challenges as opportunities for growth.

Jack started by listing his accomplishments and strengths, which helped him recognize his capabilities and build confidence. He also redefined his goals to align with his current situation, breaking them down into smaller, achievable steps. Instead of viewing his workload as an insurmountable burden, Jack began to see it as a series of manageable tasks that he could tackle one by one.

Shifting perspective involves adopting a more balanced and objective view of a situation. One effective technique is cognitive reframing, which involves changing the way you interpret and think about a challenge. For example, if you're feeling stressed about a presentation, reframe it as an opportunity to showcase your skills and knowledge rather than a source of pressure.

Another approach is to practice gratitude, which helps shift your focus from what is overwhelming to what is positive in your life. By regularly acknowledging and appreciating the things you're grateful for, you can reduce feelings of emotional overwhelm and maintain a more balanced perspective.

Developing a growth mindset also contributes to shifting your perspective. A growth mindset involves viewing challenges as opportunities for learning and development rather than as threats. By embracing this mindset, you can approach difficulties with curiosity and resilience, viewing them as chances to build new skills and grow as a person.

Balancing Emotions in High-Stress Situations: Practical Strategies to Maintain Composure When Stakes Are High

In high-stress situations, maintaining emotional balance is crucial for effective decision-making and performance. The ability to stay composed under pressure allows us to handle challenges with clarity and poise, making it easier to navigate difficult circumstances and achieve our goals.

Consider the example of Maria, a healthcare worker who frequently faced high-stress situations in the emergency room. During particularly intense moments, such as handling multiple critical patients simultaneously, Maria needed to maintain her composure to provide effective care and support to her team.

Maria used several practical strategies to balance her emotions in these high-stress situations. One strategy involved using grounding techniques, such as focusing on her breath or physical sensations, to stay centered and calm. She also practiced time management and prioritization to ensure that she addressed the most urgent needs first while maintaining a clear plan of action.

Another effective strategy is to use visualization techniques to prepare for high-stress situations. Visualization involves mentally rehearsing how you will handle a challenging scenario, which helps you build confidence and reduce anxiety. For example, if you have an upcoming presentation, visualize yourself speaking confidently and handling questions effectively. This mental rehearsal helps you approach the situation with greater composure.

Developing effective coping strategies, such as deep breathing exercises or progressive muscle relaxation, also contributes to emotional balance in high-stress situations. These techniques help calm the body and mind, reducing the physical symptoms of stress and allowing you to approach challenges with greater clarity and focus.

Additionally, maintaining a strong support network can help you manage stress and maintain emotional balance. Having friends, family, or colleagues to turn to during high-stress periods provides emotional support and practical assistance, helping you navigate challenges more effectively.

Conclusion

Building emotional resilience is a key component of emotional regulation and overall well-being. By strengthening mental fortitude, shifting perspectives, and balancing emotions in high-stress situations, we enhance our ability to navigate life's challenges with grace and composure. These strategies help us recover from adversity, manage stress effectively, and maintain a balanced outlook, enabling us to approach difficulties with confidence and resilience.

Through consistent practice and self-awareness, we can develop the emotional resilience needed to handle life's ups and downs with strength and poise. By applying these techniques, we build a foundation for emotional well-being that supports our personal and professional success, allowing us to thrive even in the face of adversity.

Handling Negative Emotions Constructively

Handling negative emotions constructively is a crucial aspect of emotional regulation. Emotions like anger, anxiety, and sadness, while natural, can become overwhelming if not managed effectively. Learning to address these emotions in a healthy and productive way not only improves our emotional well-being but also enhances our ability to cope with life's challenges. This section explores strategies for managing anger and frustration, overcoming anxiety and fear, and transforming sadness into personal growth.

Managing Anger and Frustration:
Healthy Outlets for Anger and Ways to Reduce Its Intensity

Anger and frustration are powerful emotions that, if not managed properly, can lead to destructive outcomes and hinder our relationships and well-being. Constructively handling these emotions involves finding healthy outlets and strategies to reduce their intensity.

Take the story of Alex, a project manager who often felt frustrated with his team's performance. This frustration sometimes turned into anger, which impacted his interactions with colleagues and the overall team morale. Recognizing the need to manage his anger more constructively, Alex began exploring various strategies to address his emotions in a healthier way.

One effective approach Alex discovered was to engage in physical activities such as running or practicing martial arts. Physical exercise helps release pent-up energy and reduces the physiological symptoms associated with anger, such as increased heart rate and muscle tension. For Alex, regular exercise became a productive outlet for his frustration, allowing him to calm down and approach situations with a clearer mind.

Another strategy Alex employed was mindfulness and deep-breathing exercises. By practicing mindfulness, Alex learned to observe his anger without judgment, allowing him to acknowledge the emotion without letting it control his actions. Deep-breathing techniques helped him manage the immediate physiological responses of anger, such as rapid breathing and elevated heart rate. By taking a few moments to breathe deeply and focus on his breath, Alex was able to reduce the intensity of his anger and respond more thoughtfully.

In addition to physical activities and mindfulness, Alex found that addressing the root causes of his frustration was essential. Open communication with his team and setting clear expectations helped mitigate some of the sources of his anger. By identifying and addressing these underlying issues,

Alex was able to reduce his overall frustration and improve his interactions with his colleagues.

Managing anger and frustration involves finding healthy outlets, practicing mindfulness, and addressing underlying issues. By adopting these strategies, we can handle these emotions more constructively, preventing them from negatively impacting our well-being and relationships.

Overcoming Anxiety and Fear: Addressing and Reducing Anxiety Through Emotional Intelligence

Anxiety and fear are common emotional experiences that can significantly impact our daily lives and decision-making. Overcoming these emotions involves using emotional intelligence to address and reduce their impact effectively.

Consider the experience of Lisa, a college student who struggled with anxiety before exams. Her fear of failure often led to excessive stress and impacted her performance. To address her anxiety, Lisa turned to emotional intelligence strategies that helped her manage her fears and approach her exams with greater confidence.

One approach Lisa found helpful was cognitive restructuring, which involves challenging and changing negative thought patterns. When Lisa noticed herself ruminating on worst-case scenarios, she used cognitive restructuring to reframe her thoughts. Instead of thinking, "I'm going to fail this exam," Lisa reminded herself of her preparation and past successes. This shift in perspective helped reduce her anxiety and build her confidence.

Lisa also practiced relaxation techniques such as progressive muscle relaxation and guided imagery. Progressive muscle relaxation involves tensing and then relaxing different muscle groups to release physical tension associated with anxiety. Guided imagery involves visualizing a peaceful and calming scene, which helps distract from anxious thoughts and promotes relaxation.

In addition to these techniques, Lisa developed a structured study plan that included breaks and self-care activities. By organizing her study time and incorporating relaxation breaks, she was able to manage her anxiety more effectively and maintain a sense of balance. The structured approach also helped Lisa feel more in control and less overwhelmed.

Overcoming anxiety and fear involves using cognitive restructuring to challenge negative thoughts, practicing relaxation techniques, and adopting a structured approach to manage stress. By applying these emotional intelligence strategies, we can address anxiety and fear more effectively, improving our ability to navigate challenging situations with confidence and composure.

Transforming Sadness into Growth: How to Channel Sadness into Emotional and Personal Development

Sadness, while a challenging emotion, can also be a powerful catalyst for emotional and personal growth. Transforming sadness into growth involves understanding and channeling the emotion in a way that contributes to our development and well-being.

Consider the story of John, who experienced profound sadness after a breakup. Initially, John felt overwhelmed by the sense of loss and heartache. However, he recognized that this sadness presented an opportunity for personal growth. Instead of dwelling on his pain, John decided to use this experience as a chance to reflect on his life and priorities.

John began by exploring his feelings through journaling. Writing about his emotions allowed him to process his sadness and gain insights into his needs and desires. Through this reflective process, John discovered patterns in his relationships and personal goals that he wanted to address. This self-awareness helped him identify areas for personal growth and set new objectives for himself.

John also sought support from friends and a therapist, which provided him with different perspectives and emotional support. Talking about his experiences and receiving feedback from others helped John gain clarity and develop coping strategies. This support network played a crucial role in his healing process and personal development.

Additionally, John used his experience to engage in activities that aligned with his values and passions. He took up new hobbies, such as volunteering and pursuing creative projects, which helped him find fulfillment and purpose beyond the sadness. By channeling his emotions into constructive activities, John was able to turn his sadness into a source of personal growth and positive change.

Transforming sadness into growth involves reflecting on the emotion, seeking support, and engaging in activities that align with your values and passions. By approaching sadness with a mindset of growth and self-discovery, we can use this emotion as a catalyst for positive change and personal development.

Conclusion

Handling negative emotions constructively is essential for maintaining emotional well-being and navigating life's challenges effectively. By managing anger and frustration through healthy outlets and mindfulness, overcoming anxiety and fear with emotional intelligence strategies, and transforming sadness into personal growth, we can address these emotions in a way that supports our overall well-being and development.

These strategies enable us to approach negative emotions with greater awareness and resilience, turning potentially destructive feelings into opportunities for growth and positive change. Through consistent practice and self-awareness, we can develop the skills needed to handle negative emotions constructively, enhancing our emotional regulation and overall quality of life.

The Empathy Advantage—Deepening Connections

Understanding the Core of Empathy

Empathy is a fundamental aspect of emotional intelligence that profoundly influences how we connect with others. It involves understanding and sharing the feelings of another person, creating deeper and more meaningful relationships. This section explores the essence of empathy, how the brain processes empathetic responses, and the role of emotional mirroring in strengthening connections.

What Is Empathy? The Difference Between Empathy, Sympathy, and Compassion

Empathy, sympathy, and compassion are often used interchangeably, but they represent different aspects of how we respond to others' emotions. Understanding these distinctions is crucial for developing genuine connections and providing meaningful support.

Empathy is the ability to understand and share the feelings of another person. It involves putting yourself in someone else's shoes and experiencing their emotions from their perspective. For example, if a friend is grieving the loss of a loved one, empathy allows you to feel their sadness and offer support that acknowledges their pain.

Sympathy, on the other hand, is feeling pity or sorrow for someone else's misfortune. It involves acknowledging another person's situation but from a more detached standpoint. For instance, expressing sympathy might involve saying, "I'm sorry to hear about your loss," without necessarily feeling the depth of the other person's emotions.

Compassion goes a step further by combining empathy with a desire to alleviate the suffering of others. It involves not only feeling for someone but also taking action to support or help them. For instance, after expressing sympathy for a friend's loss, compassion might involve offering practical help, such as preparing meals or providing a listening ear.

Take the example of Emma, a teacher who noticed that a student was struggling with anxiety. Emma demonstrated empathy by engaging in conversations with the student, understanding their fears, and providing emotional support. Her approach was different from mere sympathy, as she actively sought to understand the student's experience and offer relevant help. This empathetic connection allowed Emma to build a stronger relationship with the student and offer meaningful support.

Understanding the differences between empathy, sympathy, and compassion helps us respond more effectively to others' emotions and build more genuine connections. While sympathy and compassion are important, empathy forms the core of how we connect with others on a deeper emotional level.

The Neuroscience of Empathy: Exploring How the Brain Processes Empathetic Responses

The ability to empathize is rooted in the brain's complex neural networks. Neuroscience has revealed that specific brain regions are involved in processing empathetic responses, allowing us to connect with and understand others' emotions.

One of the key brain areas involved in empathy is the **mirror neuron system**. These neurons activate both when we perform an action and when we observe someone else performing the same action. For example, if you see someone smiling, your mirror neurons fire in a way that mirrors their smile, helping you experience their positive emotions. This mirroring process is fundamental to our ability to empathize and connect with others.

Another important brain region in empathy is the **empathy network**, which includes the **anterior insula** and the **anterior cingulate cortex**. The anterior insula helps us perceive and process bodily sensations related to emotions, while the anterior cingulate cortex is involved in understanding the emotional states of others. Together, these areas contribute to our ability to feel and respond to others' emotions.

Consider the story of Raj, a counselor who specialized in helping individuals cope with trauma. Raj's ability to empathize with his clients was rooted in his brain's empathy network. When a client shared a painful experience, Raj's mirror neurons and empathy network activated, allowing him to deeply understand and connect with the client's emotions. This neural process enabled Raj to provide more effective support and build trust with his clients.

The neuroscience of empathy highlights the biological basis of our emotional connections and the importance of developing our empathetic abilities. By understanding how the brain processes empathy, we can enhance our ability to connect with others and respond to their emotions more effectively.

The Importance of Emotional Mirroring: How We Reflect Others' Emotions and Build Stronger Bonds

Emotional mirroring is the process of reflecting and sharing the emotions of others, which plays a crucial role in building strong interpersonal connections. When we mirror others' emotions, we create a sense of understanding and validation that deepens our relationships.

Take the example of Laura, a manager who noticed that her team was feeling stressed and demotivated. To address this, Laura actively engaged in emotional mirroring by acknowledging her team's feelings and reflecting their emotions in her responses. During team meetings, Laura would express understanding by saying things like, "I can see that everyone is feeling overwhelmed by the current workload." This acknowledgment helped her team feel heard and validated, which improved their morale and trust in Laura's leadership.

Emotional mirroring involves several key components: **active listening**, **emotional validation**, and **non-verbal cues**. Active listening means fully focusing on the speaker, understanding their message, and responding appropriately. Emotional validation involves acknowledging and accepting the other person's feelings without judgment. Non-verbal cues, such as facial expressions and body language, also play a role in mirroring emotions and building connections.

Effective emotional mirroring requires mindfulness and sensitivity. By paying attention to others' emotional states and reflecting those emotions in a supportive and understanding manner, we create a stronger bond and foster more meaningful relationships. This practice not only enhances our ability to connect with others but also improves our overall communication and interpersonal skills.

Incorporating emotional mirroring into our interactions helps us build deeper connections and respond to others' needs more effectively. By recognizing and reflecting the emotions of those around us, we create an environment of empathy and support that strengthens our relationships and fosters mutual understanding.

Conclusion

Understanding the core of empathy is essential for deepening connections and building meaningful relationships. By differentiating empathy from sympathy and compassion, exploring the neuroscience of empathetic responses, and recognizing the importance of emotional mirroring, we enhance our ability to connect with others on a deeper level.

Empathy forms the foundation of strong interpersonal relationships, allowing us to understand and share the feelings of others. Through the lens of neuroscience, we see how our brains are wired to connect emotionally, while emotional mirroring provides practical strategies for reflecting and validating others' emotions. By cultivating empathy, we improve our relationships, enhance our communication, and foster a greater sense of understanding and connection in our personal and professional lives.

Enhancing Empathy in Everyday Life

Empathy is not just an innate ability but also a skill that can be cultivated and refined through deliberate practice. Enhancing empathy in everyday interactions involves active listening, recognizing emotional cues, and developing genuine curiosity about others' experiences. This section explores practical strategies to deepen our empathetic connections with others in our daily lives.

Active Listening: How Listening Without Judgment Can Deepen Understanding

Active listening is a cornerstone of effective communication and empathy. It involves fully concentrating on what the other person is saying, without letting our own judgments or assumptions interfere. This type of listening fosters a deeper understanding and connection by validating the speaker's feelings and experiences.

Consider the story of Anna, a team leader who noticed that one of her team members, Mark, seemed disengaged during meetings. Rather than making assumptions or jumping to conclusions, Anna decided to practice active listening to understand what was going on with Mark. During a one-on-one meeting, Anna made a conscious effort to listen attentively, maintaining eye contact and avoiding interruptions.

Anna's approach involved several key elements of active listening: she refrained from immediately offering solutions or advice, instead focusing on understanding Mark's perspective. She used reflective statements, such as, "It sounds like you've been feeling overwhelmed with the new project deadlines," to confirm her understanding of his emotions. By validating Mark's feelings and allowing him to express his concerns without judgment, Anna created a supportive environment where Mark felt heard and valued.

Active listening not only helps us gain a clearer understanding of others' emotions but also builds trust and rapport. When people feel that their thoughts and feelings are genuinely heard, they are more likely to open up and engage in meaningful conversations. This deeper understanding enhances our ability to respond empathetically and strengthen our relationships.

Incorporating active listening into our interactions involves setting aside our own biases, practicing patience, and focusing entirely on the speaker. By giving our full attention and reflecting on what is being communicated, we deepen our empathetic connections and foster more meaningful and supportive relationships.

Recognizing Emotional Cues: Reading Body Language and Emotional Signals in Conversations

Recognizing emotional cues is a crucial aspect of empathy that involves interpreting non-verbal signals to understand others' feelings. Our body language, facial expressions, and tone of voice often convey more about our emotions than our words alone. Being attuned to these cues allows us to respond more empathetically and connect with others on a deeper level.

Imagine the scenario of James, a friend who noticed that his colleague, Laura, seemed distressed despite her attempts to mask it with a smile. James observed subtle signs of her distress, such as clenched fists, furrowed brows, and a tense posture. Recognizing these emotional cues, James decided to gently ask Laura if she was okay and offered a listening ear.

Laura's response revealed that she was indeed struggling with a challenging project and felt overwhelmed. James's ability to read her non-verbal signals allowed him to offer timely support and show empathy, even though Laura hadn't explicitly expressed her feelings.

Developing the skill of recognizing emotional cues involves paying close attention to body language and non-verbal signals during conversations. Common cues include changes in facial expressions, posture, eye contact, and tone of voice. For example, if someone's shoulders are slumped and they speak with a subdued tone, it may indicate sadness or fatigue.

By honing our ability to read these emotional signals, we can respond more effectively to others' needs and emotions. This skill enhances our empathetic interactions by allowing us to provide support and understanding even when emotions are not overtly expressed.

Developing Curiosity in Others' Experiences: How Being Genuinely Interested in Others Fosters Empathy

Cultivating curiosity about others' experiences involves a genuine interest in understanding their perspectives, feelings, and life situations. This curiosity goes beyond surface-level interactions and seeks to explore the deeper aspects of others' lives, fostering a stronger empathetic connection.

Take the example of Sarah, who worked in a diverse team with colleagues from various cultural backgrounds. Rather than relying on assumptions or stereotypes, Sarah approached her interactions with genuine curiosity about her colleagues' experiences and perspectives. She asked open-ended questions about their cultural practices, personal experiences, and views on different topics.

Sarah's approach of asking thoughtful questions and showing a genuine interest in her colleagues' stories helped her build deeper relationships and foster a more inclusive and empathetic work environment. Her curiosity allowed her to understand the unique challenges and perspectives of her colleagues, which in turn enhanced her ability to connect with and support them.

Developing curiosity involves actively seeking to learn more about others' experiences and perspectives. It requires asking open-ended questions, listening attentively to their responses, and demonstrating a willingness to understand their viewpoints. This genuine interest not only deepens our empathy but also enriches our interactions and relationships.

By fostering curiosity about others, we create opportunities for more meaningful connections and build a greater understanding of their experiences. This approach helps bridge gaps in communication, promotes inclusivity, and strengthens our empathetic abilities.

Conclusion

Enhancing empathy in everyday life involves active listening, recognizing emotional cues, and developing genuine curiosity about others' experiences. These practices help us deepen our understanding of others' emotions, strengthen our connections, and respond more effectively to their needs.

Active listening enables us to fully engage with others' perspectives, while recognizing emotional cues allows us to interpret non-verbal signals and provide timely support. Developing curiosity about others fosters deeper connections and enriches our interactions by exploring their unique experiences and viewpoints.

By incorporating these strategies into our daily interactions, we cultivate stronger and more empathetic relationships, improving our overall communication and emotional intelligence. This enhanced empathy not only benefits our personal connections but also contributes to a more compassionate and supportive environment in our personal and professional lives.

Empathy in Conflict Resolution

Empathy plays a vital role in resolving conflicts and managing disputes. By understanding and acknowledging the emotions and perspectives of all parties involved, we can navigate conflicts more effectively and work towards mutually beneficial solutions. This section explores how empathy helps us see both sides of a conflict, defuse tensions, and build collaborative solutions.

Seeing Both Sides of Conflict: Using Empathy to Understand Both Perspectives in Disputes

Conflicts often arise from misunderstandings and differing viewpoints. To resolve these disputes effectively, it's essential to understand and appreciate both sides of the conflict. Empathy allows us to put ourselves in the shoes of others, gaining insight into their feelings, motivations, and concerns.

Take the case of Michael and Lisa, two colleagues who found themselves at odds over a project deadline. Michael believed that Lisa's approach to the project was too slow, while Lisa felt that Michael's expectations were unrealistic. The conflict was escalating, and productivity was suffering.

To address the issue, Michael decided to use empathy to understand Lisa's perspective. He initiated a calm conversation, during which he actively listened to Lisa's concerns about the project timeline and the challenges she was facing. By acknowledging her difficulties and expressing a willingness to understand her viewpoint, Michael gained insight into why she was struggling.

Similarly, Lisa made an effort to understand Michael's urgency and the pressures he was under. She learned that his concerns about the deadline were driven by higher management's expectations and project deliverables.

Through this empathetic approach, both Michael and Lisa were able to see each other's perspectives and recognize the underlying reasons for their disagreements. Understanding both sides allowed them to address the root causes of the conflict and work towards a resolution that considered both of their needs and concerns.

Seeing both sides of a conflict involves actively listening, validating each party's feelings, and gaining insight into their perspectives. By employing empathy in this manner, we can better understand the complexities of the dispute and develop more effective solutions.

Defusing Tensions with Empathy: How Recognizing Emotions Can Calm Heated Situations

Conflicts often lead to heightened emotions and increased tension. Empathy can play a crucial role in calming these situations by recognizing and addressing the emotions at play. When we acknowledge and validate the feelings of those involved, we create a more constructive environment for resolution.

Consider the example of Rachel, a team leader who was mediating a heated argument between two team members, John and Sarah. The argument had escalated to raised voices and defensiveness, making it challenging to find a resolution.

Rachel decided to use empathy to defuse the tension. She began by acknowledging the emotions of both John and Sarah, saying, "I can see that both of you are feeling frustrated and upset right now." By validating their feelings, Rachel created an atmosphere of respect and understanding.

Rachel then encouraged John and Sarah to express their emotions and concerns without judgment. She facilitated a dialogue where each person could share their perspective while actively listening to the other's point of view. By recognizing and addressing the emotions driving their responses, Rachel helped reduce the intensity of the conflict and fostered a more open and constructive conversation.

Empathy in conflict resolution involves acknowledging and validating the emotions of those involved, which can help reduce defensiveness and create a more cooperative environment. By addressing the emotional aspects of the conflict, we pave the way for more effective communication and problem-solving.

Building Collaborative Solutions: Leveraging Emotional Insight to Find Win-Win Outcomes

Empathy not only helps us understand different perspectives but also enables us to find collaborative solutions that benefit all parties involved. By leveraging emotional insight, we can identify common ground and work towards win-win outcomes.

Consider the case of a project team facing disagreements over resource allocation. The team members had differing priorities, and the conflict was affecting their productivity. To resolve the issue, the team leader, Emma, employed empathy to build a collaborative solution.

Emma started by facilitating a discussion where each team member could express their priorities and concerns. By using empathy, she acknowledged the emotional and practical factors influencing each person's perspective. For example, Emma recognized that some team members were motivated by personal career goals, while others were focused on meeting project deadlines.

With this understanding, Emma guided the team towards a collaborative solution that addressed everyone's needs. She proposed a revised resource allocation plan that balanced individual priorities with project requirements. Additionally, Emma encouraged team members to support one another in achieving their goals, fostering a sense of teamwork and shared responsibility.

By leveraging emotional insight and focusing on common goals, Emma was able to build a solution that satisfied all parties and enhanced team cohesion. This approach not only resolved the conflict but also improved overall team dynamics and productivity.

Building collaborative solutions involves using empathy to understand the needs and motivations of all parties, identifying common ground, and working together to find mutually beneficial outcomes. By approaching conflicts with emotional insight, we can create solutions that foster cooperation and strengthen relationships.

Conclusion

Empathy is a powerful tool in conflict resolution, helping us navigate disputes by understanding different perspectives, defusing tensions, and building collaborative solutions. By seeing both sides of a conflict, we gain insight into the underlying issues and develop more effective resolutions. Recognizing and addressing emotions during conflicts helps create a more constructive environment for communication and problem-solving.

Empathy enables us to build collaborative solutions that consider the needs and motivations of all parties involved. By leveraging emotional insight, we can find win-win outcomes that strengthen relationships and improve overall dynamics.

Incorporating empathy into conflict resolution not only enhances our ability to address disputes effectively but also fosters a more compassionate and cooperative approach to problem-solving. Through empathetic engagement, we build stronger connections, improve communication, and create more harmonious and productive environments.

Social Skills—Mastering Emotional Intelligence in Relationships

Building Stronger Relationships Through EQ

Social skills are integral to successful relationships, both personal and professional. Mastering emotional intelligence (EQ) enhances our ability to connect with others, build trust, and navigate the complexities of social interactions. This section delves into how trust and emotional honesty, compassion, and respecting emotional boundaries contribute to stronger and more fulfilling relationships.

Trust and Emotional Honesty: How Being Emotionally Open Builds Trust in Relationships

Trust is the foundation of any meaningful relationship, and emotional honesty plays a crucial role in establishing and maintaining that trust. Being open and authentic about our feelings fosters a deeper connection and builds mutual respect.

Consider the relationship between Mia and her colleague, Tom. Mia had been working closely with Tom on a high-stakes project. Initially, their interactions were professional but somewhat guarded. Mia noticed that their collaboration lacked the depth needed to effectively tackle challenges.

To build a stronger connection, Mia decided to practice emotional honesty. During a team meeting, she openly shared her concerns about the project's direction and her own stress levels. She said, "I've been feeling overwhelmed by the tight deadlines and wanted to let you know that I'm struggling with balancing this with my other responsibilities."

Tom's response was immediate. He appreciated Mia's openness and shared his own challenges with the project. This exchange of emotions created a space of mutual understanding and trust. By being emotionally honest, Mia and Tom were able to communicate more effectively, collaborate more closely, and support each other through the project's demands.

Emotional honesty involves expressing our true feelings and being transparent about our experiences. It requires vulnerability and courage but leads to deeper and more authentic relationships. When we share our emotions openly, we invite others to do the same, which strengthens trust and fosters a more supportive and empathetic connection.

The Role of Compassion in Social Interactions: Cultivating Compassion to Strengthen Connections

Compassion goes beyond empathy by incorporating a desire to alleviate the suffering of others. Cultivating compassion in our social interactions enhances our ability to connect with others and build stronger relationships.

Imagine the story of Carlos, a manager who noticed that one of his team members, Jenna, was having a difficult time at work. Jenna had been facing personal challenges that were affecting her performance and mood. Carlos decided to approach the situation with compassion.

Instead of reprimanding Jenna for her performance issues, Carlos took the time to understand her situation. He expressed his concern by saying, "I've noticed that you seem to be going through a tough time. Is there anything I can do to support you?" Carlos offered flexible work arrangements and additional resources to help Jenna manage her workload.

Carlos's compassionate approach not only helped Jenna navigate her challenges but also strengthened their professional relationship. Jenna felt valued and supported, which improved her engagement and performance. Carlos's compassion demonstrated that he cared about Jenna's well-being beyond just her work performance.

Compassion involves actively seeking to understand and support others in their times of need. By showing empathy and taking practical steps to help, we build stronger and more trusting relationships. Compassion enhances our ability to connect with others on a deeper level and fosters a positive and supportive environment.

Respecting Emotional Boundaries: Understanding the Importance of Personal Emotional Space

Respecting emotional boundaries is crucial for maintaining healthy and balanced relationships. Each person has their own emotional space and limits, and recognizing and honoring these boundaries contributes to mutual respect and trust.

Consider the scenario of Julia and her friend, Rachel. Julia had been going through a challenging time and needed space to process her emotions. However, Rachel, concerned about Julia, frequently reached out and tried to offer advice and support.

Julia appreciated Rachel's concern but felt overwhelmed by the constant inquiries and suggestions. She needed time alone to reflect and manage her feelings. Julia decided to communicate her need for space by saying, "I really appreciate your support, but I need some time to myself right now. I promise I'll reach out when I'm ready to talk."

Rachel respected Julia's boundaries and gave her the space she needed. This respect allowed Julia to process her emotions at her own pace without feeling pressured. When Julia was ready to talk, she felt more comfortable and open with Rachel, strengthening their friendship.

Respecting emotional boundaries involves understanding and honoring the limits of others in terms of emotional support and interaction. It requires recognizing when someone needs space and being sensitive to their needs. By respecting these boundaries, we foster healthier and more respectful relationships.

Conclusion

Building stronger relationships through emotional intelligence involves cultivating trust and emotional honesty, practicing compassion, and respecting emotional boundaries. These elements contribute to deeper connections and more fulfilling interactions.

Trust and emotional honesty are foundational for meaningful relationships. By being open and authentic, we build mutual respect and understanding. Compassion enhances our ability to connect with others and support them through challenges, strengthening our relationships. Respecting emotional boundaries ensures that our interactions are respectful and considerate, contributing to healthier and more balanced connections.

Incorporating these principles into our social interactions not only enhances our relationships but also enriches our overall emotional intelligence. By practicing trust, compassion, and respect, we create a more supportive and empathetic environment that fosters stronger and more meaningful connections with those around us.

Effective Communication with EQ

Effective communication is a cornerstone of strong relationships and successful interactions. Mastering emotional intelligence (EQ) in communication involves understanding and leveraging nonverbal cues, giving and receiving feedback empathetically, and managing conflicts constructively. This section delves into how these elements enhance our ability to communicate effectively and build stronger connections.

The Power of Nonverbal Communication: Using Body Language, Tone, and Facial Expressions Effectively

Nonverbal communication plays a significant role in how our messages are received and understood. Our body language, tone of voice, and facial expressions often convey more than words alone. Being mindful of these nonverbal cues enhances our ability to communicate with empathy and clarity.

Consider the story of Emma, who was having a difficult conversation with her friend, Alex, about a misunderstanding that had caused tension between them. Emma was aware that her tone and body language could impact the outcome of the discussion. She made a conscious effort to maintain a calm and open posture, use a gentle tone, and convey her feelings through expressive facial expressions.

During the conversation, Emma noticed that Alex's body language was closed off, with crossed arms and a tense posture. Recognizing these nonverbal signals, Emma adjusted her approach by leaning in slightly and using more open and reassuring gestures. She also made sure her tone remained calm and supportive, saying, "I understand that this situation has been frustrating, and I really want us to work through it together."

By being aware of and adjusting her nonverbal communication, Emma was able to create a more supportive and empathetic atmosphere. Alex responded positively to the open and reassuring signals, which helped de-escalate the tension and foster a more productive conversation.

The power of nonverbal communication lies in its ability to enhance or undermine the message we are trying to convey. By using body language, tone, and facial expressions effectively, we can reinforce our verbal messages and create a more empathetic and understanding communication environment.

Emotionally Intelligent Feedback: Giving and Receiving Feedback in a Constructive, Empathetic Manner

Feedback is an essential component of communication that can significantly impact relationships and professional interactions. Emotionally intelligent feedback involves delivering and receiving feedback in a manner that is constructive, empathetic, and supportive.

Take the example of Jordan, a team leader who needed to give feedback to a team member, Sam, about his recent performance. Jordan recognized that delivering feedback effectively required more than just stating the issues; it needed to be done in a way that was constructive and empathetic.

Jordan approached Sam with a focus on specific behaviors rather than personal attributes. He used "I" statements to express his observations and concerns, saying, "I noticed that there were some missed deadlines in your recent reports, and I wanted to discuss how we can address these issues together." Jordan also balanced the feedback with positive reinforcement, acknowledging Sam's strengths and contributions.

When receiving feedback, Sam practiced active listening and asked clarifying questions to fully understand Jordan's perspective. He also expressed appreciation for the constructive nature of the feedback, which helped him stay open and engaged in the discussion.

Emotionally intelligent feedback involves being clear, specific, and supportive. By focusing on behaviors rather than personal traits and balancing constructive criticism with positive reinforcement, we create an environment where feedback is seen as a tool for growth rather than a personal attack. Receiving feedback with an open mind and a willingness to improve further enhances our ability to communicate effectively.

Conflict Management in Relationships: Using Emotional Intelligence to Manage and Resolve Interpersonal Conflicts

Conflicts are a natural part of relationships and interactions, but how we manage and resolve them can greatly impact the quality of our relationships. Emotional intelligence plays a crucial role in navigating conflicts constructively and finding solutions that address the needs of all parties involved.

Consider the situation of Lisa and James, who were colleagues working on a project with conflicting ideas about the project's direction. The disagreement had led to increased tension and ineffective collaboration. To address the conflict, Lisa and James decided to use their emotional intelligence skills.

Lisa began by acknowledging James's perspective and expressing her own feelings in a non-confrontational manner. She used "I" statements to describe how the conflict was affecting her and suggested a collaborative approach to finding a solution. Lisa said, "I feel that our different ideas are causing some tension, and I believe that if we work together to find a compromise, we can improve our project."

James responded by actively listening to Lisa's concerns and expressing his own views without becoming defensive. He acknowledged the validity of Lisa's feelings and proposed a brainstorming session to explore potential solutions. By focusing on common goals and maintaining a respectful tone, Lisa and James were able to de-escalate the conflict and collaborate more effectively.

Conflict management with emotional intelligence involves recognizing and addressing emotions, maintaining a respectful and open dialogue, and working towards solutions that meet the needs of all parties. By approaching conflicts with empathy and a focus on collaboration, we can resolve disputes constructively and strengthen our relationships.

Conclusion

Effective communication with emotional intelligence encompasses understanding and utilizing nonverbal communication, giving and receiving feedback empathetically, and managing conflicts constructively.

These elements enhance our ability to connect with others, build stronger relationships, and navigate interpersonal interactions more effectively.

The power of nonverbal communication lies in its ability to reinforce or undermine our verbal messages. By using body language, tone, and facial expressions thoughtfully, we create a more empathetic and supportive communication environment. Emotionally intelligent feedback involves delivering and receiving feedback in a constructive and supportive manner, which fosters growth and improves interactions.

Conflict management with emotional intelligence involves recognizing and addressing emotions, maintaining respect, and working towards collaborative solutions. By incorporating these principles into our communication practices, we enhance our relationships and create a more positive and productive interaction environment.

Mastering these aspects of emotional intelligence in communication not only improves our relationships but also contributes to our overall effectiveness in personal and professional interactions. By being mindful of our nonverbal cues, practicing empathetic feedback, and managing conflicts with emotional intelligence, we build stronger, more meaningful connections and navigate social interactions with greater ease and understanding.

Navigating Difficult Social Situations

Navigating challenging social situations requires a nuanced approach that leverages emotional intelligence (EQ) to manage difficult personalities, set boundaries empathetically, and maintain emotional balance in group settings. This section explores practical strategies for handling these complex scenarios, fostering healthier interactions, and preserving emotional well-being.

Dealing with Difficult Personalities: How to Manage Emotionally Charged Interactions with Challenging People

Interactions with difficult personalities can be emotionally taxing and challenging. Whether it's a confrontational coworker, a critical friend, or a demanding family member, managing these interactions requires a combination of patience, empathy, and strategic communication.

Consider the situation of Sarah, who worked with a colleague, Mike, known for his abrasive and confrontational demeanor. Sarah found that her interactions with Mike often left her feeling frustrated and stressed. Recognizing the need for a strategic approach, Sarah decided to apply emotional intelligence to manage her interactions more effectively.

When faced with Mike's confrontational behavior, Sarah practiced active listening and empathy. Instead of reacting defensively, she focused on understanding his perspective and acknowledging his feelings. She would say, "I see that you're really passionate about this issue, and I want to understand your concerns better."

Sarah also used assertive communication to set clear expectations and boundaries. She calmly expressed her own views and preferences without escalating the conflict. For example, she might say, "I understand your point of view, but I'd like to discuss this in a way that's respectful for both of us."

By managing her reactions and using empathetic listening, Sarah was able to maintain her composure and reduce the emotional intensity of her interactions with Mike. This approach not only improved her interactions with him but also contributed to a more positive work environment.

Dealing with difficult personalities involves maintaining emotional control, practicing empathy, and using assertive communication to navigate challenging interactions. By applying these strategies, we can manage emotionally charged situations more effectively and foster more constructive relationships.

Setting Boundaries with Empathy: Balancing Assertiveness and Compassion When Establishing Personal Boundaries

Setting boundaries is essential for maintaining healthy relationships and emotional well-being. However, doing so with empathy requires balancing assertiveness with compassion, ensuring that our needs are met while respecting the feelings of others.

Take the case of Linda, who was struggling with a friend, Mark, who frequently imposed on her time and energy. Linda felt overwhelmed by Mark's constant demands and needed to set boundaries to protect her well-being. To do so effectively, she decided to approach the situation with empathy.

Linda began by having an open and honest conversation with Mark. She expressed her feelings using "I" statements to avoid sounding accusatory. For instance, she said, "I've been feeling really stretched thin with my commitments, and I need to set some limits on how often I can help out."

Linda also acknowledged Mark's needs and emotions. She said, "I understand that you're going through a tough time, and I want to be supportive. However, I need to balance my own needs as well." By expressing her empathy and understanding, Linda was able to set boundaries without causing offense or damaging the friendship.

Balancing assertiveness with compassion involves clearly communicating our needs while considering the feelings of others. By approaching boundary-setting with empathy, we protect our own well-being while maintaining respect and understanding in our relationships.

Maintaining Emotional Balance in Group Settings: Strategies for Navigating Group Dynamics While Preserving Emotional Health

Group settings often present a mix of personalities, opinions, and dynamics that can impact our emotional well-being. Navigating these dynamics effectively requires maintaining emotional balance while engaging constructively with others.

Consider the experience of James, who was part of a project team with diverse and sometimes conflicting viewpoints. The group dynamics often led to disagreements and stress, affecting James's emotional health. To maintain his balance, James employed several strategies rooted in emotional intelligence.

First, James practiced self-awareness by monitoring his own emotional responses and recognizing when he was becoming overwhelmed. He used mindfulness techniques, such as deep breathing and taking short breaks, to manage his stress and maintain composure.

Second, James focused on fostering positive interactions by encouraging open communication and collaboration. He made an effort to listen actively to his colleagues' viewpoints and contribute constructively to discussions. By maintaining a positive and collaborative attitude, James helped create a more harmonious group environment.

Finally, James set personal boundaries to protect his emotional health. He communicated his limits and priorities clearly and respectfully, ensuring that he did not overextend himself or compromise his well-being for the sake of group dynamics.

Maintaining emotional balance in group settings involves self-awareness, positive engagement, and setting personal boundaries. By employing these strategies, we can navigate group dynamics more effectively and preserve our emotional health while contributing to a productive and supportive group environment.

Conclusion

Navigating difficult social situations with emotional intelligence involves managing challenging personalities, setting boundaries empathetically, and maintaining emotional balance in group settings. These strategies enhance our ability to handle complex interactions, build stronger relationships, and preserve our emotional well-being.

Dealing with difficult personalities requires a combination of patience, empathy, and assertive communication. By managing our reactions and practicing empathetic listening, we can reduce the emotional intensity of challenging interactions. Setting boundaries with empathy involves balancing assertiveness with compassion, ensuring that our needs are met while respecting the feelings of others.

Maintaining emotional balance in group settings involves self-awareness, positive engagement, and setting personal boundaries. By applying these principles, we can navigate group dynamics more effectively and contribute to a supportive and productive environment.

Mastering these aspects of emotional intelligence in social situations not only improves our interactions but also enhances our overall effectiveness in building and maintaining meaningful relationships. By approaching difficult situations with empathy and emotional insight, we create more positive and constructive interactions, leading to healthier and more fulfilling connections with others.

Conflict Resolution—Turning Disagreements into Growth

Understanding the Emotional Roots of Conflict

Conflict is an inevitable part of human interaction, and understanding its emotional underpinnings is crucial for resolving disagreements constructively. This section explores the emotional triggers behind conflicts, recognizes escalation patterns, and examines the role of ego in disputes. By delving into these aspects, we can transform conflicts into opportunities for growth and mutual understanding.

The Emotional Triggers Behind Conflict: How Unrecognized Emotions Lead to Clashes

Conflicts often arise from deep-seated emotions that are not immediately apparent. These unrecognized emotions can fuel disagreements and contribute to misunderstandings. By identifying and addressing these underlying emotional triggers, we can prevent and resolve conflicts more effectively.

Consider the case of Jane and her colleague, Mike, who frequently clashed during team meetings. On the surface, their disagreements seemed to stem from differing opinions on project strategies. However, a closer look revealed that their conflicts were rooted in unrecognized emotions.

Jane discovered that her frustration with Mike was partly due to her feelings of inadequacy and insecurity about her role in the team. She felt that Mike's assertiveness was overshadowing her contributions, which triggered a defensive response. Mike, on the other hand, felt threatened by Jane's critical feedback, which tapped into his own insecurities about his competence.

Understanding these emotional triggers was key to resolving their conflicts. Jane and Mike decided to have an open conversation about their feelings and frustrations. By acknowledging their underlying emotions, they were able to address the root causes of their disagreements and find common ground.

Unrecognized emotions, such as insecurity, fear, or inadequacy, can escalate conflicts when they are not addressed. By becoming aware of these emotions and discussing them openly, we can prevent misunderstandings and build a foundation for more constructive interactions.

Recognizing Escalation Patterns: Identifying When Emotions Cause Conflicts to Intensify

Conflicts often follow a pattern of escalation, where emotions escalate and exacerbate the disagreement. Recognizing these escalation patterns can help us intervene early and manage conflicts before they spiral out of control.

Take the example of Alex and Rachel, who were close friends but had a recurring issue with managing their finances together. Their discussions about budgeting often turned into heated arguments. Alex noticed that their conflicts followed a predictable pattern: a minor disagreement would quickly escalate into a full-blown argument.

Alex decided to analyze their interactions to understand the escalation pattern. He observed that the arguments tended to intensify when emotions such as frustration and resentment were triggered. For instance, when Rachel felt that Alex was not contributing his fair share, her frustration would build up and lead to a more intense conflict.

By recognizing this pattern, Alex and Rachel implemented strategies to manage their emotions and prevent escalation. They agreed to take breaks during heated discussions and reconvene when they were calmer. They also focused on addressing specific issues rather than letting emotions dictate the conversation.

Recognizing escalation patterns involves paying attention to how conflicts develop and identifying when emotions begin to intensify. By intervening early and using strategies to manage emotions, we can prevent conflicts from escalating and work towards more constructive resolutions.

The Role of Ego in Conflict: How Emotional Intelligence Helps Mitigate Ego-Driven Disputes

Ego often plays a significant role in conflicts, driving individuals to defend their position and prioritize personal pride over resolution. Emotional intelligence can help mitigate ego-driven disputes by fostering empathy and focusing on mutual understanding.

Consider the conflict between two senior executives, Lisa and Tom, who were competing for a major promotion. Their disagreements were marked by strong egos and a desire to prove their superiority. The conflict became increasingly contentious as each executive sought to assert their dominance.

Emotional intelligence helped Lisa and Tom navigate their ego-driven disputes. They decided to focus on the shared goals and interests of their organization rather than their personal ambitions. By shifting their perspective from competition to collaboration, they were able to approach the conflict with a more balanced and empathetic mindset.

Lisa and Tom also engaged in active listening and acknowledged each other's strengths and contributions. They recognized that their ego-driven disputes were hindering their ability to work together effectively. By addressing their ego-driven motivations and focusing on common objectives, they were able to resolve their conflict and find a mutually beneficial solution.

The role of ego in conflict involves the desire to protect one's self-image and assert dominance. Emotional intelligence helps mitigate these ego-driven disputes by fostering empathy, focusing on shared goals, and promoting collaborative problem-solving. By addressing the underlying ego issues, we can resolve conflicts more effectively and build stronger, more cooperative relationships.

Conclusion

Understanding the emotional roots of conflict involves identifying emotional triggers, recognizing escalation patterns, and addressing the role of ego. By exploring these aspects, we can transform conflicts into opportunities for growth and mutual understanding.

Emotional triggers, such as insecurity and fear, can lead to conflicts when they are not addressed. Recognizing and discussing these underlying emotions helps prevent misunderstandings and build a foundation for constructive interactions. Escalation patterns, where conflicts intensify due to unmanaged emotions, can be mitigated by intervening early and using strategies to manage emotions. By recognizing these patterns, we can prevent conflicts from spiraling out of control.

Ego often drives conflicts, leading individuals to prioritize personal pride over resolution. Emotional intelligence helps mitigate ego-driven disputes by fostering empathy and focusing on mutual understanding. By addressing ego issues and promoting collaboration, we can resolve conflicts more effectively and strengthen relationships.

Mastering these aspects of emotional intelligence in conflict resolution enhances our ability to manage disagreements constructively and turn them into opportunities for growth. By understanding the emotional roots of conflict and applying emotional intelligence, we create a more positive and supportive environment for resolving disputes and building stronger connections.

The Power of Emotional De-Escalation

Emotional de-escalation is a crucial skill in conflict resolution that involves calming tensions, fostering understanding, and transforming negative energy into productive solutions. This section explores the power of emotional de-escalation by examining techniques for staying centered, employing empathetic listening, and redirecting negative energy into constructive outcomes. By mastering these strategies, we can manage conflicts more effectively and turn disagreements into opportunities for growth.

Using Calm to Control the Situation: Staying Emotionally Centered to De-Escalate Tension

In high-stress situations, maintaining emotional composure can significantly influence the outcome of a conflict. Staying calm allows us to manage our reactions and create an environment where productive dialogue can occur. This technique not only helps de-escalate tension but also sets a positive tone for conflict resolution.

Consider the experience of Raj, who found himself in a heated argument with a client over a project deadline. The client was visibly frustrated and raised their voice, which threatened to escalate the conflict further. Recognizing the importance of staying calm,

Raj took a deep breath and focused on maintaining a composed demeanor.

Raj's calm presence had a calming effect on the client. By managing his own emotional response, Raj was able to address the client's concerns without adding to the tension. He used a steady, reassuring tone and avoided reacting defensively. For instance, he said, "I understand that this situation is frustrating, and I want to work together to find a solution that meets your needs."

Staying emotionally centered allows us to control the situation and prevent conflicts from escalating. By maintaining composure, we can facilitate more effective communication and create a space for resolution. This approach not only helps manage the immediate conflict but also fosters a more positive and respectful interaction.

Empathetic Listening During Conflict:

How to Use Empathy to Diffuse Emotional Disagreements

Empathetic listening involves fully engaging with the other person's perspective and emotions, which can be particularly effective in diffusing emotional disagreements. By validating and understanding the other person's feelings, we can de-escalate tensions and foster mutual respect.

Take the example of Maya and Carlos, who were having a disagreement about a shared project. Carlos was upset because he felt Maya had not taken his input into account. During their conversation, Maya practiced empathetic listening by focusing on Carlos's emotions and perspective.

Maya listened attentively, nodding and making verbal affirmations such as, "I hear you, and I understand that you feel your input wasn't considered." She refrained from interrupting and made an effort to reflect back Carlos's feelings. For example, she said, "It sounds like you're feeling frustrated because you wanted to make sure your ideas were included in the final plan."

By employing empathetic listening, Maya was able to diffuse Carlos's frustration and create a more constructive dialogue. Carlos felt heard and validated, which helped lower his emotional intensity and made it easier for them to work together towards a solution.

Empathetic listening during conflict involves actively engaging with the other person's emotions and perspective. By validating their feelings and demonstrating understanding, we can diffuse disagreements and build a more collaborative approach to resolving the issue.

Redirecting Negative Energy into Solutions: Turning Emotional Intensity into Productive Outcomes

Emotional intensity can often lead to unproductive conflicts if not managed properly. Redirecting negative energy into solutions involves channeling the emotional charge into constructive actions and problem-solving. This approach helps turn conflicts into opportunities for finding mutually beneficial outcomes.

Consider the situation of Emma and John, who were arguing over resource allocation for a team project. The discussion had become heated, with both parties expressing frustration and dissatisfaction. Recognizing the need to redirect the negative energy, Emma suggested taking a step back and focusing on finding a solution.

Emma proposed a brainstorming session where both she and John could collaboratively explore different options for resource allocation. She framed the discussion in terms of shared goals and potential benefits. For instance, she said, "Instead of focusing on our disagreements, let's look at how we can optimize our resources to achieve the best results for the project."

By redirecting their emotional intensity into problem-solving, Emma and John were able to move past their conflict and develop a more effective resource allocation plan. This approach not only resolved their disagreement but also led to a more productive and collaborative outcome.

Redirecting negative energy into solutions involves focusing on constructive actions and problem-solving. By channeling emotional intensity into productive outcomes, we can turn conflicts into opportunities for growth and achieve more positive results.

Conclusion

The power of emotional de-escalation involves using calm to control the situation, employing empathetic listening, and redirecting negative energy into solutions. Mastering these techniques enhances our ability to manage conflicts constructively and transform disagreements into opportunities for growth.

Staying emotionally centered helps control the situation and prevent conflicts from escalating. By maintaining composure, we create an environment where effective communication and resolution can occur. Empathetic listening involves fully engaging with the other person's emotions and perspective, which helps diffuse disagreements and foster mutual respect.

Redirecting negative energy into solutions involves channeling emotional intensity into constructive actions and problem-solving. By focusing on collaborative outcomes, we turn conflicts into opportunities for positive results and growth.

Mastering emotional de-escalation techniques enhances our conflict resolution skills and contributes to healthier, more productive interactions. By applying these principles, we can manage conflicts more effectively, build stronger relationships, and create a more positive and supportive environment.

Collaborating for Solutions

Collaboration is at the heart of effective conflict resolution, and it involves creatively harnessing emotions to find solutions, compromising with emotional intelligence, and turning conflicts into opportunities for growth. This section delves into how emotionally-informed problem solving, empathetic compromise, and reflective learning can transform conflicts into constructive experiences. By mastering these strategies, we can enhance our ability to resolve disagreements and strengthen our relationships.

Emotionally-Informed Problem Solving: How Emotions Can Guide Creative Solutions During Conflict

Emotions play a crucial role in problem solving, offering valuable insights into our needs and perspectives. When approached constructively, these emotional insights can guide us towards creative and effective solutions during conflicts.

Take the example of Lara and Sam, who were at an impasse over the direction of a community project. Both were passionate about their ideas but found themselves locked in a contentious debate. Recognizing the potential of their emotions, they decided to use their feelings as a guide to find a solution.

Lara and Sam took time to articulate their emotional stakes in the project. Lara shared her feelings of frustration about not being heard, while Sam expressed his concern that his vision was being dismissed. By understanding each other's emotional investments, they realized that their strong feelings were rooted in a shared commitment to the project's success.

With this emotional awareness, they began brainstorming solutions that addressed their underlying concerns. They used their emotions as a springboard for creativity, exploring ways to integrate both of their ideas into a cohesive plan. For instance, they proposed a phased approach that would incorporate both visions while allowing for flexibility and adaptation.

Emotionally-informed problem solving involves using emotions as a guide to uncover underlying needs and perspectives. By leveraging emotional insights, we can generate creative solutions that address the core issues of a conflict and promote collaboration.

Compromising with Emotional Intelligence: Finding Common Ground Without Sacrificing Emotional Needs

Compromise is often necessary in conflict resolution, but it requires balancing differing needs and perspectives while maintaining emotional integrity. Compromising with emotional intelligence involves finding common ground that respects both parties' emotional needs and contributes to a mutually satisfying resolution.

Consider the case of Tom and Rachel, who were negotiating a work schedule. Tom wanted to work flexible hours to accommodate his personal commitments, while Rachel preferred a more structured schedule to ensure team consistency. Both were emotionally invested in their preferences, and reaching a compromise required careful consideration of their needs.

Tom and Rachel decided to approach the compromise with emotional intelligence. They began by expressing their feelings and needs openly. Tom explained how flexible hours would help him manage work-life balance, while Rachel shared her concerns about maintaining team cohesion with a less structured schedule.

Together, they explored options that could meet both of their needs. They proposed a hybrid schedule that offered flexibility while maintaining core hours for team meetings and collaboration. This compromise allowed Tom to manage his personal commitments while ensuring that Rachel's need for consistency was met.

Compromising with emotional intelligence involves finding solutions that respect both parties' emotional needs and perspectives. By approaching compromise with empathy and open communication, we can reach agreements that satisfy both parties and strengthen the relationship.

Turning Conflict into Learning Opportunities: Using Emotional Insights to Foster Personal and Relational Growth After Conflict

Conflicts can be valuable learning experiences if approached with a mindset of growth and reflection. By using emotional insights gained from the conflict, we can foster personal and relational growth, transforming disagreements into opportunities for improvement.

Consider the experience of Amanda and Brian, who had a heated argument about their differing approaches to a family vacation. The conflict revealed underlying issues related to communication and expectations. After resolving the immediate disagreement, Amanda and Brian reflected on the emotional insights gained during the conflict.

Amanda realized that her frustration stemmed from feeling unheard and unappreciated, while Brian recognized that his defensive reactions were rooted in a fear of failing to meet expectations. By discussing these insights openly, they were able to address their communication patterns and develop strategies for better understanding each other's needs.

Amanda and Brian used the lessons learned from their conflict to enhance their relationship. They committed to regular check-ins to discuss their expectations and preferences, and they practiced active listening to ensure that both voices were heard. This reflective approach helped them build a stronger and more resilient relationship.

Turning conflict into learning opportunities involves using emotional insights to understand and improve communication and relational dynamics. By reflecting on the lessons learned and applying them to future interactions, we can foster personal and relational growth and build more meaningful connections.

Conclusion

Collaborating for solutions involves using emotions to guide problem solving, compromising with emotional intelligence, and turning conflicts into opportunities for growth. Mastering these strategies enhances our ability to resolve disagreements constructively and strengthen our relationships.

Emotionally-informed problem solving leverages emotional insights to guide creative solutions, addressing the underlying needs and perspectives of all parties. Compromising with emotional intelligence involves finding common ground that respects both parties' emotional needs, promoting mutual satisfaction and understanding.

Turning conflict into learning opportunities involves reflecting on emotional insights to foster personal and relational growth. By using the lessons learned from conflicts to improve communication and relational dynamics, we build stronger and more resilient relationships.

By applying these principles, we can navigate conflicts more effectively, turning disagreements into opportunities for growth and enhancing our ability to collaborate and build meaningful connections.

Emotional Resilience— Thriving Amidst Adversity

The Building Blocks of Emotional Resilience

Emotional resilience is the ability to adapt and thrive amidst adversity, and it involves a blend of mental toughness, adaptability, and optimism. This section explores the building blocks of emotional resilience by distinguishing it from mental toughness, developing an adaptive mindset, and understanding the role of optimism. By mastering these elements, we can enhance our ability to navigate challenges and maintain emotional strength.

Mental Toughness vs. Emotional Resilience: Understanding the Key Differences and Why Resilience Matters More

Mental toughness and emotional resilience are often used interchangeably, but they represent different concepts. Mental toughness refers to the ability to endure difficult situations through sheer willpower and determination. It is about withstanding pressure and persisting in the face of challenges. Emotional resilience, on the other hand, involves the capacity to adapt to stress and adversity, recover from setbacks, and maintain emotional equilibrium.

Consider the story of Sarah, a corporate manager facing significant challenges due to a major project failure. Sarah's mental toughness allowed her to push through the initial shock and continue working hard to rectify the situation. However, it was her emotional resilience that enabled her to fully recover and grow from the experience.

While mental toughness involves enduring hardship, emotional resilience encompasses the ability to bounce back and thrive. Resilience matters more because it involves a holistic approach to handling adversity, including emotional adaptability, recovery, and personal growth. Sarah's journey illustrates that resilience not only helps us cope with challenges but also allows us to transform them into opportunities for development and improvement.

Developing an Adaptive Mindset: How to Remain Flexible and Emotionally Steady During Challenges

An adaptive mindset is crucial for emotional resilience, as it enables us to remain flexible and steady in the face of challenges. Developing this mindset involves embracing change, staying open to new possibilities, and managing our emotional responses effectively.

Consider John, who faced a significant career setback when his startup failed. Initially, John was overwhelmed by disappointment and uncertainty. However, he recognized the need to adapt to the changing circumstances. Instead of clinging to his original plans, John chose to view the failure as an opportunity for growth.

John adopted an adaptive mindset by focusing on what he could learn from the experience and exploring new avenues. He sought feedback from mentors, updated his skills, and adjusted his career goals based on the lessons learned. This flexibility allowed him to navigate his career transition with greater ease and resilience.

Developing an adaptive mindset involves cultivating a willingness to embrace change and view challenges as opportunities for learning and growth. By remaining open to new possibilities and managing our emotional responses effectively, we can maintain emotional steadiness and thrive amid adversity.

The Role of Optimism in Emotional Resilience: How Cultivating Hope Can Enhance Emotional Strength

Optimism plays a vital role in emotional resilience by fostering hope and a positive outlook, which enhances our ability to cope with adversity. Cultivating optimism involves maintaining a hopeful perspective, even in the face of difficulties, and focusing on potential positive outcomes.

Take the example of Laura, who faced a series of personal and professional setbacks, including health issues and job loss. Despite these challenges, Laura chose to maintain an optimistic outlook. She regularly reminded herself of her strengths and past successes, and she visualized positive outcomes for her future.

Laura's optimism helped her persevere through tough times and maintain her emotional resilience. By focusing on the potential for positive change and believing in her ability to overcome obstacles, she was able to navigate her challenges with greater emotional strength.

Optimism involves cultivating hope and focusing on potential positive outcomes, even in difficult circumstances. By maintaining a hopeful perspective and reinforcing our belief in our ability to overcome challenges, we enhance our emotional resilience and ability to thrive amidst adversity.

Conclusion

The building blocks of emotional resilience include understanding the differences between mental toughness and emotional resilience, developing an adaptive mindset, and cultivating optimism. Mastering these elements enhances our ability to navigate challenges, maintain emotional steadiness, and thrive amidst adversity.

Mental toughness involves enduring hardship, while emotional resilience encompasses the capacity to recover and grow from setbacks. Resilience matters more because it involves a holistic approach to handling adversity, including emotional adaptability and personal growth.

Developing an adaptive mindset enables us to remain flexible and open to new possibilities during challenges. By managing our emotional responses and viewing difficulties as opportunities for learning, we can maintain emotional steadiness and navigate transitions more effectively.

Optimism plays a crucial role in emotional resilience by fostering hope and a positive outlook. Cultivating optimism enhances our ability to cope with adversity and reinforces our belief in our capacity to overcome obstacles.

By applying these principles, we can build emotional resilience and thrive amidst adversity. Embracing the building blocks of resilience allows us to navigate challenges with greater strength, adaptability, and optimism, transforming difficulties into opportunities for growth and development.

Overcoming Setbacks with Emotional Intelligence

Overcoming setbacks is a critical aspect of emotional resilience, and it requires harnessing emotional intelligence to recover from failure, manage grief, and turn mistakes into growth opportunities. This section explores how emotionally intelligent people navigate setbacks, cope with significant loss, and reframe failures as pathways to personal and professional development. By mastering these strategies, we can build resilience and emerge stronger from adversity.

Bouncing Back from Failure: How Emotionally Intelligent People Recover from Defeat

Failure is an inevitable part of life, but how we respond to it can significantly impact our ability to bounce back. Emotionally intelligent individuals understand that setbacks are not reflections of their worth but rather opportunities for growth and learning. They approach failure with resilience, using their emotional insights to recover and move forward.

Consider the experience of Michael, an entrepreneur whose startup faced a major financial setback. The failure was devastating, and Michael initially felt disheartened and uncertain about his future. However, he used his emotional intelligence to process his feelings constructively.

Michael began by acknowledging his emotions without judgment. He allowed himself to feel disappointment and frustration but did not let these feelings dictate his actions. Instead, he used his emotional insights to identify what went wrong and what he could learn from the experience.

Michael sought feedback from mentors and peers, focusing on understanding the root causes of the failure. He reframed the setback as a valuable learning opportunity, using the insights gained to refine his approach and develop a more robust business plan. By leveraging his emotional intelligence, Michael was able to recover from defeat and continue pursuing his entrepreneurial goals with renewed determination.

Bouncing back from failure involves acknowledging and processing emotions constructively, learning from the experience, and using insights to improve future efforts. Emotionally intelligent individuals use their resilience to turn setbacks into opportunities for growth and development.

Managing Grief and Loss: Emotional Intelligence Strategies to Cope with Significant Loss

Grief and loss are profound challenges that require emotional intelligence to navigate effectively. Emotionally intelligent individuals understand the importance of acknowledging and managing their emotions during times of loss, using strategies to cope and find meaning in their experiences.

Consider the case of Julia, who lost her father unexpectedly. The grief she experienced was overwhelming, and she struggled to find a way to cope with the profound sense of loss. Julia turned to emotional intelligence strategies to manage her grief and support her healing process.

Julia began by allowing herself to fully experience her emotions, including sadness, anger, and confusion. She recognized that these feelings were natural and important parts of the grieving process. Julia sought support from friends, family, and a therapist, creating a network of emotional support to help her navigate her grief.

Additionally, Julia used reflective practices to process her emotions and find meaning in her loss. She engaged in journaling and meditation to explore her feelings and memories of her father. This process helped her gain perspective and find solace in the positive impact her father had on her life.

Managing grief and loss involves acknowledging and processing emotions, seeking support, and finding meaningful ways to cope. By using emotional intelligence strategies, we can navigate the complexities of grief and build resilience in the face of significant loss.

Turning Failure into Growth: How to Reframe Mistakes as Learning Opportunities

Reframing failure as a learning opportunity is a powerful strategy for turning setbacks into growth. Emotionally intelligent individuals use their experiences with failure to gain insights, make improvements, and develop greater resilience. This approach involves shifting our perspective to view mistakes as valuable lessons rather than sources of discouragement.

Consider the story of Ella, a project manager who experienced a significant failure when a major project did not meet its objectives. Initially, Ella felt disheartened and questioned her abilities. However, she chose to reframe the failure as an opportunity for growth and learning.

Ella began by analyzing the project to identify what went wrong and what could be improved. She gathered feedback from her team and stakeholders, focusing on understanding the factors that contributed to the failure. Ella used this information to develop a comprehensive plan for addressing the issues and preventing similar mistakes in the future.

By reframing the failure as a learning opportunity, Ella was able to turn her setback into a catalyst for personal and professional development. She implemented new strategies, improved her project management skills, and approached future challenges with greater confidence and resilience.

Turning failure into growth involves reframing setbacks as opportunities for learning and improvement. By using our experiences with failure to gain insights and make positive changes, we build resilience and enhance our ability to navigate future challenges effectively.

Conclusion

Overcoming setbacks with emotional intelligence involves bouncing back from failure, managing grief and loss, and turning mistakes into growth opportunities. Mastering these strategies enhances our ability to navigate adversity and build emotional resilience.

Bouncing back from failure requires acknowledging and processing emotions constructively, learning from setbacks, and using insights to improve future efforts. Emotionally intelligent individuals use their resilience to recover from defeat and continue pursuing their goals with renewed determination.

Managing grief and loss involves acknowledging and processing emotions, seeking support, and finding meaningful ways to cope. By using emotional intelligence strategies, we can navigate the complexities of grief and build resilience in the face of significant loss.

Turning failure into growth involves reframing setbacks as learning opportunities and using our experiences to gain insights and make improvements. By adopting this perspective, we can turn failures into catalysts for personal and professional development.

By applying these principles, we can overcome setbacks with emotional intelligence, build resilience, and thrive amidst adversity. Embracing these strategies allows us to navigate challenges more effectively, recover from failures, and turn setbacks into opportunities for growth and development.

Emotional Coping Strategies for Everyday Stress

Navigating everyday stress requires effective emotional coping strategies that help us maintain balance and resilience amidst daily challenges. This section explores building a daily emotional resilience practice, developing emotional anchors, and balancing work, relationships, and personal life. By integrating these strategies into our lives, we can enhance our ability to manage stress and sustain emotional well-being.

Building a Daily Emotional Resilience Practice: Incorporating Mindfulness and Reflection into Your Routine

Creating a daily emotional resilience practice involves integrating mindfulness and reflection into your routine to manage stress and maintain emotional balance. This practice helps us stay grounded, enhance self-awareness, and respond to daily challenges with greater ease.

Consider the experience of Alex, a busy executive managing multiple responsibilities at work and home. Alex often felt overwhelmed by the demands of his job, which affected his emotional well-being. To address this, Alex decided to incorporate mindfulness and reflection into his daily routine.

Every morning, Alex dedicated 10 minutes to mindfulness meditation, focusing on his breath and being present in the moment. This practice helped him start the day with a sense of calm and clarity. Additionally, Alex set aside time each evening to reflect on his day, acknowledging his accomplishments and identifying areas where he felt stress or imbalance.

By integrating these practices into his routine, Alex developed greater emotional resilience and improved his ability to manage daily stress. Mindfulness and reflection became essential tools for staying centered and maintaining emotional balance amidst his busy life.

Building a daily emotional resilience practice involves incorporating mindfulness and reflection into your routine to enhance self-awareness and manage stress. By dedicating time to these practices, we can foster emotional well-being and navigate daily challenges with greater resilience.

Developing Emotional Anchors: Identifying the Things That Keep You Emotionally Grounded

Emotional anchors are practices, activities, or relationships that help us stay grounded and maintain emotional balance during stressful times. Identifying and nurturing these anchors is crucial for managing everyday stress and sustaining emotional resilience.

Take the example of Maya, a teacher who often felt stressed by the demands of her job and personal life. Maya recognized the need for emotional anchors to help her stay grounded amidst her busy schedule. She identified several key anchors that provided her with stability and comfort.

Maya's emotional anchors included spending time with her family, engaging in creative hobbies such as painting, and maintaining a regular exercise routine. These activities provided her with a sense of joy and relaxation, helping her recharge and manage stress more effectively.

By actively nurturing her emotional anchors, Maya was able to maintain emotional balance and resilience. Her anchors provided her with a reliable source of support and comfort, helping her navigate the stresses of daily life with greater ease.

Developing emotional anchors involves identifying and nurturing the practices, activities, or relationships that help you stay grounded and balanced. By integrating these anchors into your life, you can enhance your ability to manage stress and maintain emotional resilience.

Balancing Work, Relationships, and Personal Life: How to Stay Emotionally Balanced in All Areas of Your Life

Achieving balance between work, relationships, and personal life is essential for maintaining emotional well-being and managing stress effectively. It requires thoughtful planning, prioritization, and self-care to ensure that each area of your life receives the attention and care it needs.

Consider the experience of Jordan, a software developer who struggled to balance the demands of his job with his personal and family life. Jordan felt overwhelmed by work-related stress and found it challenging to dedicate quality time to his relationships and personal interests.

To address this, Jordan implemented several strategies to achieve balance. He began by setting clear boundaries between work and personal time, ensuring that he did not bring work-related stress into his home life. Jordan also prioritized quality time with his family, scheduling regular activities and check-ins to strengthen his relationships.

Additionally, Jordan made time for personal hobbies and self-care, such as reading and exercising, to recharge and maintain his well-being. By balancing his work, relationships, and personal life, Jordan was able to manage stress more effectively and maintain emotional resilience.

Balancing work, relationships, and personal life involves thoughtful planning and prioritization to ensure that each area receives the attention it deserves. By setting boundaries, nurturing relationships, and engaging in self-care, you can maintain emotional balance and manage stress effectively.

Conclusion

Emotional coping strategies for everyday stress include building a daily emotional resilience practice, developing emotional anchors, and balancing work, relationships, and personal life. Mastering these strategies enhances our ability to manage stress and maintain emotional well-being.

Building a daily emotional resilience practice involves incorporating mindfulness and reflection into your routine to enhance self-awareness and manage stress. By dedicating time to these practices, you can foster emotional well-being and navigate daily challenges with greater resilience.

Developing emotional anchors involves identifying and nurturing the practices, activities, or relationships that help you stay grounded and balanced. By integrating these anchors into your life, you can enhance your ability to manage stress and maintain emotional resilience.

Balancing work, relationships, and personal life requires thoughtful planning and prioritization to ensure that each area receives the attention it needs. By setting boundaries, nurturing relationships, and engaging in self-care, you can maintain emotional balance and manage stress effectively.

By applying these principles, you can enhance your emotional resilience and thrive amidst daily stressors. Integrating these strategies into your life allows you to navigate challenges with greater ease, maintain balance, and sustain emotional well-being.

Lifelong EQ—Applying Emotional Intelligence for Lasting Success

Emotional Intelligence for Professional Success

Emotional intelligence (EQ) plays a pivotal role in achieving professional success, influencing how we lead teams, negotiate effectively, and advance in our careers. This section delves into how emotional intelligence enhances leadership skills, improves negotiation outcomes, and supports career growth. By applying EQ principles in these areas, we can achieve lasting success and build meaningful professional relationships.

Using EQ to Lead Teams Effectively: How Emotional Intelligence Enhances Leadership Skills

Leadership is not just about setting direction and making decisions; it's also about understanding and managing the emotions of yourself and others. Emotionally intelligent leaders are adept at creating a positive work environment, fostering team cohesion, and inspiring performance.

Consider the leadership approach of Emma, a project manager at a tech company. Emma's team faced significant challenges during a high-stakes project, and tensions were running high. Emma's emotionally intelligent approach involved recognizing and addressing the emotional climate of her team. She actively listened to her team members' concerns, validated their feelings, and provided support and encouragement.

Emma used her emotional intelligence to build strong relationships with her team, creating an environment where open communication and mutual respect were prioritized. By understanding and managing the emotions of her team, Emma was able to diffuse conflicts, motivate her team, and guide them toward successful project completion.

Emotionally intelligent leadership involves recognizing and managing both your own emotions and those of your team members. By fostering an emotionally supportive environment, you enhance team performance and achieve better results.

Emotional Intelligence in Negotiation: Leveraging EQ to Win Negotiations and Build Stronger Professional Relationships

Negotiation is a critical skill in the professional world, and emotional intelligence can significantly impact the outcome. EQ allows negotiators to understand and manage their own emotions, read the emotions of others, and navigate the negotiation process with empathy and effectiveness.

Take the example of David, a sales executive who frequently negotiates contracts with clients. David's success in negotiations is partly due to his high emotional intelligence. He approaches each negotiation with an understanding of the client's needs and concerns, using empathy to build rapport and trust.

David's emotionally intelligent approach involves active listening and responding to the client's emotional cues. By acknowledging their perspectives and addressing their concerns, he creates a collaborative atmosphere that facilitates agreement. David also manages his own emotions, remaining calm and composed even in high-pressure situations.

By leveraging emotional intelligence in negotiations, you can build stronger professional relationships, achieve favorable outcomes, and enhance your overall effectiveness as a negotiator.

The Role of EQ in Career Growth: How Emotional Intelligence Impacts Promotions, Networking, and Career Success

Emotional intelligence is a key factor in career growth, influencing promotions, networking opportunities, and overall career success. EQ helps individuals navigate the complexities of the workplace, build meaningful professional relationships, and position themselves for advancement.

Consider the career trajectory of Sofia, a marketing professional who leveraged her emotional intelligence to advance in her career. Sofia's ability to understand and manage her emotions, as well as those of her colleagues, played a crucial role in her professional success.

Sofia's emotional intelligence helped her build a strong professional network, as she was able to connect with others on a personal level and understand their needs and motivations. Her empathetic approach made her a valued team member and a natural choice for leadership roles.

Additionally, Sofia's ability to manage her own emotions and respond to workplace challenges with resilience contributed to her career advancement. Her emotional intelligence was recognized by her superiors, leading to promotions and increased responsibilities.

Emotional intelligence impacts career growth by enhancing networking opportunities, supporting effective communication, and positioning you for professional advancement. By applying EQ principles in your career, you can build meaningful relationships, navigate workplace dynamics, and achieve lasting success.

Conclusion

Applying emotional intelligence in the professional realm involves using EQ to lead teams effectively, excel in negotiations, and drive career growth. Mastering these aspects of emotional intelligence can significantly impact your success and satisfaction in the workplace.

Using EQ to lead teams involves understanding and managing emotions to create a positive work environment, foster team cohesion, and inspire performance. Emotionally intelligent leadership enhances team effectiveness and contributes to achieving better results.

In negotiations, leveraging emotional intelligence allows you to build stronger professional relationships, understand others' perspectives, and achieve favorable outcomes. EQ helps you navigate negotiations with empathy and composure, enhancing your effectiveness as a negotiator.

Emotional intelligence also plays a crucial role in career growth, influencing promotions, networking opportunities, and overall success. By applying EQ principles, you can build meaningful professional relationships, navigate workplace dynamics, and position yourself for advancement.

By integrating emotional intelligence into your professional life, you set the stage for lasting success and fulfillment. Embracing EQ principles enables you to lead with empathy, negotiate effectively, and grow your career, ultimately achieving your professional goals and building a rewarding career.

Emotional Intelligence for Personal Fulfillment

Emotional intelligence (EQ) is not only crucial for professional success but also for personal fulfillment. Applying EQ principles in our personal lives can help us live authentically, strengthen relationships, and achieve a balanced and fulfilling life. This section explores how emotional intelligence contributes to living authentically, deepening personal connections, and maintaining emotional and life balance.

Living Authentically Through Emotional Awareness: Using EQ to Align Your Life with Your Values and Passions

Living authentically involves aligning our actions and decisions with our core values and passions. Emotional awareness plays a vital role in this alignment, as it helps us understand our true selves and make choices that reflect who we are.

Consider the journey of Lisa, a graphic designer who felt unfulfilled despite a successful career. Lisa realized that her discontent stemmed from a disconnect between her work and her personal values. She decided to use her emotional intelligence to explore her feelings and uncover her true passions.

Lisa began by reflecting on her emotional responses to different aspects of her life. She noticed that she felt most energized and fulfilled when engaging in creative projects that aligned with her personal values. Through this self-awareness, Lisa recognized that her passion lay in using her design skills for social causes rather than corporate work.

By aligning her career with her values, Lisa found a renewed sense of purpose and fulfillment. She transitioned to a role with a nonprofit organization focused on environmental sustainability, where she could apply her skills to make a meaningful impact. Living authentically through emotional awareness allowed Lisa to create a career that resonated with her passions and values.

Living authentically involves using emotional awareness to align your life with your core values and passions. By understanding your true self and making choices that reflect your beliefs, you can achieve a deeper sense of fulfillment and purpose.

Strengthening Family and Personal Relationships: Applying Emotional Intelligence to Create Deeper, More Meaningful Connections

Emotional intelligence enhances our ability to build and maintain strong, meaningful relationships with family and friends. By applying EQ principles, we can improve communication, understand others' emotions, and foster deeper connections.

Take the example of Mark and Sarah, a married couple facing challenges in their relationship. They often found themselves in conflict and struggled to communicate effectively. Recognizing the need for change, they decided to apply emotional intelligence strategies to strengthen their relationship.

Mark and Sarah began by practicing active listening and empathetic communication. They made a conscious effort to understand each other's perspectives and validate their feelings. This approach helped them address underlying issues and improve their communication.

Additionally, Mark and Sarah worked on expressing their emotions openly and honestly. By sharing their thoughts and feelings with each other, they built a stronger emotional connection and resolved conflicts more effectively. Applying emotional intelligence allowed them to create a more supportive and fulfilling relationship.

Strengthening family and personal relationships involves applying emotional intelligence to improve communication, understand emotions, and build deeper connections. By fostering empathy and openness, you can create more meaningful and supportive relationships.

Achieving Emotional and Life Balance: Maintaining Long-Term Emotional Well-Being Amidst Life's Demands

Maintaining emotional and life balance is essential for long-term well-being and fulfillment. Emotional intelligence helps us manage the demands of daily life while preserving our emotional health and achieving a balanced lifestyle.

Consider the experience of Alex, a busy professional juggling work, family, and personal interests. Alex often felt overwhelmed by the demands on his time and struggled to maintain balance. He decided to use emotional intelligence strategies to manage his commitments and achieve a more balanced life.

Alex began by setting clear boundaries between work and personal time. He scheduled regular breaks and prioritized activities that contributed to his well-being, such as exercise and hobbies. Alex also made time for family and personal relationships, ensuring that these areas of his life received the attention they needed.

Additionally, Alex practiced self-care and emotional regulation techniques to manage stress and maintain balance. He engaged in mindfulness practices and reflection to stay centered and focused amidst life's demands. By incorporating these strategies, Alex achieved a greater sense of balance and emotional well-being.

Achieving emotional and life balance involves using emotional intelligence to manage daily demands, set boundaries, and prioritize self-care. By maintaining balance in all areas of your life, you can sustain long-term emotional well-being and fulfillment.

Conclusion

Applying emotional intelligence for personal fulfillment involves living authentically, strengthening relationships, and achieving emotional and life balance. Mastering these aspects of EQ enhances our ability to navigate life's challenges and build a fulfilling and meaningful life.

Living authentically through emotional awareness allows us to align our actions and decisions with our core values and passions. By understanding our true selves and making choices that reflect our beliefs, we achieve a deeper sense of purpose and fulfillment.

Strengthening family and personal relationships involves applying emotional intelligence to improve communication, understand emotions, and build meaningful connections. By fostering empathy and openness, we create supportive and fulfilling relationships.

Achieving emotional and life balance requires using emotional intelligence to manage daily demands, set boundaries, and prioritize self-care. By maintaining balance in all areas of our lives, we sustain long-term emotional well-being and fulfillment.

By integrating emotional intelligence into our personal lives, we set the stage for lasting success and happiness. Embracing EQ principles allows us to live authentically, build meaningful relationships, and achieve a balanced and fulfilling life.

A Roadmap to Continuous EQ Growth

Emotional intelligence (EQ) is not a static trait but a dynamic skill that can be developed and refined over time. Continuous growth in EQ involves lifelong learning, measuring progress, and creating actionable plans to integrate emotional intelligence practices into our daily lives. This section outlines a roadmap for ongoing EQ development, providing practical strategies for enhancing your emotional intelligence throughout your life.

Lifelong Learning and Emotional Intelligence: How to Continue Building Emotional Intelligence Throughout Your Life

Emotional intelligence is a journey of lifelong learning. Just as we evolve professionally and personally, our capacity for emotional intelligence can continue to grow and deepen with intentional effort. Embracing a mindset of continuous learning helps us adapt to changing circumstances and improve our EQ over time.

Take the example of Tom, a senior executive who recognized the importance of lifelong learning in maintaining and enhancing his emotional intelligence. Despite his experience, Tom understood that emotional intelligence was an area where he could always improve. He made a commitment to ongoing personal and professional development.

Tom pursued various learning opportunities, such as workshops, seminars, and courses focused on emotional intelligence. He also sought feedback from colleagues and mentors to gain insights into his emotional strengths and areas for growth. Tom's dedication to lifelong learning enabled him to stay attuned to his emotions, adapt to new challenges, and continue to develop his EQ.

Lifelong learning in emotional intelligence involves actively seeking opportunities to expand your knowledge and skills. By engaging in ongoing education and self-reflection, you can continue to enhance your EQ and navigate life's challenges with greater effectiveness.

Measuring Your EQ Progress: Tools and Assessments to Track and Grow Your Emotional Intelligence

Tracking and measuring your emotional intelligence progress is essential for understanding your growth and identifying areas for improvement. Various tools and assessments can help you gauge your EQ and guide your development efforts.

Consider the experience of Emily, a manager who wanted to track her progress in emotional intelligence. Emily used several tools to assess her EQ, including self-assessment questionnaires, 360-degree feedback from colleagues, and emotional intelligence tests.

Emily's self-assessment questionnaires allowed her to evaluate her emotional awareness, self-regulation, empathy, and social skills. The 360-degree feedback provided valuable insights from peers and subordinates, highlighting areas where she excelled and where she could improve. Additionally, Emily utilized emotional intelligence tests to gain a comprehensive understanding of her EQ strengths and weaknesses.

By regularly using these tools, Emily was able to monitor her progress and set targeted goals for further development. Measuring your EQ progress involves using assessments and feedback to track growth and identify areas for improvement, ensuring that you continue to enhance your emotional intelligence.

Creating a Personal EQ Action Plan: Concrete Steps for Incorporating Emotional Intelligence Practices into Everyday Life

Developing a personal EQ action plan involves setting specific, actionable steps to integrate emotional intelligence practices into your daily life. This plan helps you apply what you've learned about EQ in practical ways and fosters continuous growth.

Consider the approach of Sarah, a team leader who wanted to incorporate emotional intelligence practices into her daily routine. Sarah created a detailed action plan with concrete steps to enhance her EQ.

Sarah's action plan included setting aside time each day for self-reflection and mindfulness practices to improve her emotional awareness. She also committed to actively listening during team meetings and providing constructive feedback to foster better communication. Additionally, Sarah planned to engage in regular emotional intelligence training and seek feedback from her team to track her progress.

By following her action plan, Sarah was able to integrate emotional intelligence practices into her daily life, resulting in improved team dynamics and personal growth. Creating a personal EQ action plan involves identifying specific steps to apply EQ principles in your life, setting measurable goals, and tracking your progress to ensure continued development.

Conclusion

A roadmap to continuous EQ growth involves embracing lifelong learning, measuring progress, and creating a personal EQ action plan. By incorporating these strategies into your life, you can enhance your emotional intelligence and achieve lasting success.

Lifelong learning in emotional intelligence involves seeking opportunities for education and self-improvement. By staying committed to expanding your knowledge and skills, you can continue to develop your EQ and adapt to changing circumstances.

Measuring your EQ progress helps you track your growth and identify areas for improvement. Using tools and assessments provides valuable insights into your emotional strengths and weaknesses, guiding your development efforts.

Creating a personal EQ action plan involves setting concrete steps to integrate emotional intelligence practices into your daily routine. By implementing your action plan, you can apply EQ principles in practical ways and foster continuous growth.

By following this roadmap, you set the stage for ongoing emotional intelligence development and lasting personal and professional success. Embracing EQ as a lifelong journey allows you to navigate challenges, build meaningful relationships, and achieve fulfillment throughout your life.

www.ingramcontent.com/pod-product-compliance
Lightning Source LLC
Chambersburg PA
CBHW071053240526
45471CB00015B/1792